Holiday Baking
Cookbook

50+ Seasonal Treats to Warm Your Heart and Home:
Celebrate Winter's Joyful Moments with Merry Sweets
and Cozy Recipes
FULL COLOR EDITION

Olivia Dowson

4

Legal & Disclaimer

The information contained in this book and its contents is not designed to replace or take the place of any form of medical or professional advice; and is not meant to replace the need for independent medical, financial, legal or other professional advice or services, as may be required. The content and information in this book have been provided for educational and entertainment purposes only.

The content and information contained in this book have been compiled from sources deemed reliable, and it is accurate to the best of the Author's knowledge, information, and belief. However, the author cannot guarantee its accuracy and validity and cannot be held liable for any errors and/or omissions. Further, changes are periodically made to this book as and when needed. Where appropriate and/or necessary, you must consult a professional (including but not limited to your doctor, attorney, financial advisor or such other professional advisor) before using any of the suggested remedies, techniques, or information in this book.

Upon using the contents and information contained in this book, you agree to hold harmless the Author from and against any damages, costs, and expenses, including any legal fees potentially resulting from the application of any of the information provided by this book. This disclaimer applies to any loss, damages or injury caused by the use and application, whether directly or indirectly, of any advice or information presented, whether for breach of contract, tort, negligence, personal injury, criminal intent, or under any other cause of action.

You agree to accept all risks of using the information presented inside this book. You agree that by continuing to read this book, where appropriate and/or necessary, you shall consult a professional (including but not limited to your doctor, attorney, or financial advisor or such other advisor as needed) before using any of the suggested remedies, techniques, or information in this book.

To my family, the heart of every recipe.
For all the laughter, the hugs, and the memories made in the kitchen,
and for every time you turned simple ingredients into something
magical.
This book is for you, because every dish is sweeter when shared with you.

Table of Content

3 Gifts of Delight

4 Not just Christmas

5 Extra Delights

About Me

Hi! I'm Olivia Dowson, and I'm thrilled to share my passion for cooking with you. I live in Geneva, Illinois, a charming town where nature's beauty meets a warm community atmosphere, perfect for celebrating and sharing special moments.

Growing up in a family that cherishes traditions and the love of food, I found joy in the aromas of sweet treats that filled our home during the holidays. My parents instilled in me a love for baking, making every occasion memorable. From whipping up festive cookies to experimenting with new recipes, the kitchen has always been a space for connection and creativity.

As a mother of two wonderful children, I cherish creating that same magic in our home. We spend our days cooking together and exploring new dishes. However, I want to emphasize that the kitchen is a gathering place for everyone. Whether you're a parent, a single friend, or someone who simply enjoys gathering with loved ones, my hope is that everyone can find inspiration and joy in my recipes.

With the unwavering support of my husband and the love of my friends, I embarked on the journey to write this cookbook. It's been a labor of love, crafted with care and passion, from the recipes to the accompanying images. This book is for everyone—an invitation to celebrate not just special moments with family, but also to relish the everyday joys with friends.

I hope my recipes inspire you to create unforgettable moments with those you love, because the true magic of cooking lies in sharing experiences and enjoying the sweet results of our efforts. Whether it's a celebration or a casual dinner with friends, there's always a reason to whip up something delicious.

Join me on this journey of love and cooking, one recipe at a time!

How to use this book

While my family celebrates Christmas, this book is really meant to embrace the whole season—the months leading up to the holidays and the cozy days that follow. It's about the joy of gathering and savoring time with loved ones as we wind down the year.

This book is divided into **<u>five chapters</u>**, each offering a unique flavor of holiday baking.

The **first chapter,** Morning Breads and Pastries, is filled with recipes perfect for hosting overnight guests, festive brunches, lazy weekend mornings, and, of course, Christmas morning. You'll find classics like Cinnamon Rolls and Powdered Sugar Donuts, along with fun twists on old favorites like Cranberry and Cream Danish , Coffee-Cardamom Bread, and Panettone Scones.

Holiday Desserts is the focus of **Chapter Two,** dedicated to sweets that make holiday dinners and gatherings extra special. Inside, you'll find recipes like Carrot Cake with Caramelized Honey Buttercream; Apple, Caramel, and Rustic Apple Pie with Caramel & Hard; and Creamy Chocolate Mint Ice Cream Pie all designed to end any meal on a memorable note.

Chapter Three, Gifts from the Kitchen, is all about treats to share with neighbors, coworkers, family, and friends. Mini Fruit Cakes are a personal favorite, as are Peanut Butter Cups, Crunchy Orange-Almond Treats, and Triple Triple Chocolate Peppermint Bark—all guaranteed to spread holiday cheer.

Chapter Four, Winter Warmth, stretches the season beyond December, capturing the magic of those long, chilly January days. Here, you'll find recipes that highlight winter flavors and cozy vibes, like Crispy Blood Orange Turnovers, Tangy Lemon Pull-Apart Bread, and Decadent Hot Chocolate Cake.

Finally, **the Extras chapter** brings together foundational recipes you can use in other desserts or enjoy on their own, like Ice Cream Without the Churn, Sugared & Spiced Candied Nuts, Heavenly Pastry Cream and Silky Lemon Curd.
This book is a companion for all your holiday baking adventures, whether you're looking to create new traditions or revisit cherished ones.

Enjoy every moment, every bite, and every memory made along the way.

A Few Important Notes on Technique

General Baking Advice

When it comes to baking, patience and precision are your best friends. That's why it's so important to take the time to carefully read through the entire recipe before you begin. Every detail, every step—no matter how small—can make the difference between a good dessert and an unforgettable one. Knowing all the ingredients, the timing, and the techniques in advance will help you tackle the project with confidence and ease. Once you fully understand the recipe, that's when you can think about adding your own personal touch, making it your own, and infusing it with that special love only someone who's baking for the people they care about can add.

Measuring Flour

Throughout this book, 1 cup of flour equals about 142 grams (or 5 ounces). This is a measurement I've found after lots of trial and error. I know it might just seem like a number, but I promise you, even small variations in how much flour you use can really affect the final result. Every time I measured flour, I realized how important it is to be precise, especially when you want your baked goods to turn out light and fluffy. If I could give you one tip, it would be to always use a scale to get accurate and consistent measurements. But, if you don't have a scale on hand, the "dip and level" method will work just fine: dip your measuring cup into the bag of flour, then use the flat edge of a knife to level off the top. That way, you'll always have the right amount of flour, and your creations will turn out just the way you imagined.

Measuring Semisolids

Ingredients like yogurt, sour cream, peanut butter, and pumpkin puree can be a bit tricky to measure. They're not quite liquids, but they're not exactly solids either. For these, the best tool is a liquid measuring cup, which will give you a slightly more generous volume than a dry measuring cup. I always recommend using a liquid measuring cup for these types of ingredients, especially if you're not using a scale. Measuring these semisolid ingredients carefully will help you achieve just the right consistency for your baked goods. After all, it's these little details that are part of the magic of baking—that moment when you combine simple ingredients and create something truly special, something that brings a smile to the faces of those who get to taste it.

Just a Pinch of Salt

Though it's used in the tiniest amounts, salt plays a big role in baking. When I mention a pinch of salt in this book, I'm talking about a little more than 1/8 of a teaspoon but less than 1/4. It might seem like a small detail, but that little pinch balances the flavors and brings everything together. It's amazing how such a small thing can make such a big difference, right?

That Perfect Golden Touch – Egg Wash

To achieve that perfect golden, crisp finish on your baked goods, an egg wash is your best friend. To make it, whisk one large egg with a pinch of salt and a tablespoon of water until it's nicely blended. Brush this mix over your pastries before baking, and watch as they transform in the oven, developing a beautiful golden crust. There's something magical about seeing your baked treats take on that perfect color, isn't there?

The Secret to No-Stick Bakes – Lining Your Pans with Parchment

Parchment paper can truly be a lifesaver in the kitchen. It makes sure your cakes and breads lift out perfectly without sticking or breaking apart. For square or rectangular pans, cut two strips of parchment paper, wide enough to fit the base and long enough to hang over the sides. Lightly spray the pan with cooking spray to help the paper stick, then lay the pieces in the pan, overlapping them to cover all the sides. This simple step ensures easy removal and helps prevent those frustrating moments when your cake just won't let go!

Making Round Pans a Breeze

Round pans can seem a bit tricky, but they're a breeze once you get the hang of it. Start by cutting a circle of parchment paper to fit the bottom of the pan. Grease the sides and bottom of the pan with a generous layer of softened butter. After placing the parchment at the bottom, brush another light layer of butter on top of the paper, or spray with cooking spray. Then, toss a couple of tablespoons of flour into the pan and shake it around until the butter is evenly coated. Gently tap out any extra flour into the sink, and voilà—your pan is ready to go!

Easy Chocolate Tempering

Tempering chocolate can seem like an intimidating skill, but I promise, with a little practice, it becomes a fun and rewarding part of your kitchen adventures. Achieving that perfectly smooth, glossy chocolate is not only beautiful but adds a delightful snap to your desserts. The method I use in this book is a bit of a shortcut, but it works wonders. Slowly melt most of your chocolate, being careful not to overheat it, and then finely chop the rest. Stir the chopped chocolate into the melted portion until it's smooth and fully combined. The heat from the melted chocolate will melt the rest, giving you a silky texture. While this method isn't foolproof, it's worked for me 99% of the time. And when you see that glossy chocolate set perfectly on your treats, you'll know it was worth the effort.

The Essential Ingredients

Every recipe needs the right ingredients to truly shine. Here's a list of the staples you'll use throughout this book. Most of them should be easy to find at your local grocery store.

Dairy and Eggs – The Building Blocks of Great Baking
Butter – Butter is the soul of so many baked goods, and in this book, I always use unsalted butter. Unsalted butter gives you full control over the amount of salt in your recipes. If you prefer to use salted butter, just remember to reduce the amount of added salt a bit. It's also worth noting that European-style butter, with its higher fat content, can affect the texture of your baked goods. If a recipe calls for European butter specifically, it will be noted.

Cream Cheese – For that perfect creamy, velvety texture, cream cheese is key. I always opt for Philadelphia brand in my recipes because it strikes the perfect balance of smoothness and flavor. It's ideal for cheesecakes, frostings, and so much more.

Crème Fraîche – Crème fraîche is a lightly tangy, silky cream used to add a touch of freshness to many recipes. You'll find it used occasionally in this book, and there's even a recipe in the Extras section if you'd like to make it at home. If you prefer to buy it ready-made, I recommend Vermont Creamery for a consistently high-quality option.

Eggs – Eggs are essential in so many recipes, and here I use large, grade A eggs. In their shell, a large egg weighs about 2 oz (57 g). When recipes call for egg-rich ingredients like pastry cream, I love using farm-fresh eggs with vibrant, orange yolks. If your recipe asks for room-temperature eggs, here's a little trick: place them in warm water for about 10 minutes. This will bring them to the right temperature quickly. And if you need to separate the yolks from the whites, it's always easier to do so with cold eggs since the yolks hold their shape better.

Heavy Cream – Look for pasteurized, not ultra-pasteurized, heavy cream whenever possible, especially when making crème fraîche. This kind of cream, also known as double cream, adds that luscious richness to your recipes.

Milk – I tested every recipe in this book using whole milk. While it might seem like a small change, using low-fat milk can alter the texture and flavor of your baked goods. Whole milk adds the creamy consistency you need to get the best results.

Cooking Oils – The Subtle Stars
Canola Oil – Canola oil is one of the most versatile and neutral oils you'll use in this book. Its mild flavor makes it perfect for a wide variety of recipes. If you want an alternative, grapeseed oil is another good option with a similar neutral flavor profile.

Olive Oil – When a dish calls for a little extra depth, high-quality extra virgin olive oil is perfect. Choose a good one, and its rich, fruity flavor will shine through in your final product, adding that extra touch of magic to even the simplest recipes.

Toasted Sesame Oil – The bold, nutty flavor of toasted sesame oil is usually used in savory dishes, but I've discovered that a hint of it paired with sugar can create a wonderfully unexpected flavor combination in desserts. It's a little experiment that might just surprise and delight your taste buds!

Salts and Spices – The Flavor Enhancers
Fleur de Sel – Fleur de sel is a delicate, moist salt, perfect for sprinkling on your finished dishes as a final touch. The larger crystals dissolve slowly, leaving a subtle burst of flavor that lingers just a bit longer, making every bite a little more special.

Spices – Fresh spices can take a dish from good to extraordinary, so it's important to make sure yours are still at their best. Even though they seem to last forever, spices can lose their potency or go stale over time. Keep them stored in a cool, dry place and try to replace them every 6 months to a year for the best results.

Table Salt – In all the recipes in this book, I use regular table salt unless noted otherwise. It's a trusty staple that dissolves easily and helps balance flavors perfectly.

Sweeteners – The Heart of Sweetness
Brown Sugar – In these recipes, I used light brown sugar. It adds a subtle molasses flavor and moisture to your baked goods, which can make all the difference in cookies and cakes. While dark brown sugar can be tempting with its rich, deep flavor, it's not always the best substitute due to the higher moisture content. Stick with light brown sugar unless otherwise noted to keep that perfect balance in texture and sweetness.

Confectioners' Sugar – Also known as powdered sugar or icing sugar, this fine-textured sugar is perfect for frostings, glazes, and dusting over cookies and cakes. Its delicate texture helps give frostings that smooth, creamy consistency we all love. Plus, it dissolves easily, making it ideal for light, airy desserts that need a gentle sweetness.

Corn Syrup – Corn syrup adds a glossy finish and keeps your treats moist. For these recipes, stick with light corn syrup unless otherwise specified. Dark corn syrup has a much stronger flavor that could overpower the other ingredients in your recipe. It's best to follow the instructions to ensure your desserts come out just right.

Granulated Sugar – Commonly known as white sugar, this was my go-to for testing all the recipes in this book. It's reliable and provides a clean, straightforward sweetness. If you're using organic sugar, keep in mind that it often has a coarser texture, which might not melt as easily in batters. For a smoother result, you can pulse it in a food processor until it's finely ground.

Sanding Sugar – This is a larger-crystal sugar that's mostly used for decorating. It doesn't dissolve while baking, so it adds a fun, crunchy texture and a sparkle to cookies and cakes. It's perfect when you want to make your holiday cookies look a little more festive!

Flour – The Foundation of Every Bake

All-Purpose Flour – For all of the recipes in this book, I tested them with Gold Medal unbleached all-purpose flour. Flour is the backbone of baking, and different brands have different protein levels, which can impact the final result. I found Gold Medal to be a consistent choice for the best outcomes, but you can use your preferred brand. Just remember that a higher protein flour might give a denser result, while a lower one could make things too crumbly.

Almond Flour – This finely ground flour, made from blanched almonds, is a wonderful alternative for gluten-free baking or for adding a nutty flavor to your goods. It's available in most grocery stores or online. I love using almond flour in delicate cakes or cookies where the subtle nuttiness shines through without overpowering other flavors.

Hazelnut Flour – If you can't find hazelnut flour at your local store, don't worry. You can easily make your own by pulsing skinned hazelnuts in a food processor until finely ground. Be careful not to over-process, though, as it can turn into nut butter! Hazelnut flour adds a beautiful depth to baked goods, especially in recipes like cookies and tarts.

Leavening Agents – The Power Behind the Rise

Baking Powder – I always use non-aluminum baking powder to avoid that metallic aftertaste. It's a key ingredient to give cakes and muffins their height and fluffiness. If you're not sure if your baking powder is still fresh, add a spoonful to a cup of hot water. If it fizzes, it's still good to go. This simple test can save you from flat cakes and disappointing bakes.

Baking Soda – Baking soda is a powerful leavening agent, but it needs an acidic ingredient to work its magic. Things like buttermilk, sour cream, or even molasses help activate it, giving your baked goods their rise. If you're unsure about its freshness, you can do the same test as baking powder—just add it to some hot water and see if it bubbles.

Nuts – Bringing Out the Best Flavor

I like to toast my nuts as soon as I buy them to enhance their flavor and then store them in the freezer so they stay fresh. To toast your nuts, preheat your oven to 350°F (180°C) and spread them out in a single layer on a baking sheet lined with parchment paper. Bake for 5 to 10 minutes until they're fragrant and golden. Let them cool completely before storing in a freezer-safe bag or container. Toasted nuts add such a rich, warm flavor to baked goods, and keeping them in the freezer ensures they stay fresh and ready to use whenever inspiration strikes.

Chocolate – The Soul of Decadent Baking

Bittersweet/Semisweet Chocolate – When baking with chocolate, it's important to choose the right one. For bittersweet and semisweet chocolate, look for bars that contain between 35% and 60% cacao.

Anything over 70% can change the texture and flavor of your recipe in unexpected ways. Bittersweet and semisweet chocolates are often used interchangeably, but be mindful of the cacao content. Most recipes in this book use semisweet chocolate for its balance of sweetness and depth.

Melting Chocolate – For the best results, chop your chocolate into small pieces before melting it. This helps it melt evenly and prevents scorching. Always be careful not to let any water come in contact with your chocolate, as this can cause it to seize and turn grainy. If it does seize, try adding a tablespoon or two of hot water to bring it back. It may not always work, but it's worth trying before you start over.

Cocoa Powder – There are two main types of cocoa powder: Dutch-process and natural. Dutch-process cocoa is treated with an alkaline solution to neutralize its acids, giving it a richer color and milder flavor. Natural cocoa, on the other hand, is more acidic and has a sharper taste. In this book, I recommend using Dutch-process cocoa for its smooth flavor and deep, rich color.

White Chocolate – White chocolate is made from cocoa butter and melts more quickly than dark chocolate. Be sure to stir it often when melting, especially in the microwave, as it can burn easily. Unlike dark chocolate, white chocolate chips don't melt well, so it's best to use a high-quality white chocolate bar for the smoothest results.

Vanilla – The Fragrant Heart of Flavor
Vanilla Beans – To use a vanilla bean, slice it lengthwise and scrape out the seeds using the back of a knife or a spoon. The seeds add an intense vanilla flavor that's hard to beat. The leftover pod can be dried and ground into a powder to sprinkle over desserts or mix into sugar. It's a great way to get the most out of every bean.

Vanilla Extract – All the recipes in this book call for Natural vanilla extract. While artificial vanilla can be tempting, it just doesn't offer the same depth and warmth that real vanilla brings. Stick with the real stuff, and your baked goods will taste richer and more fragrant.

Tools of the Trade
Essential Equipment for the Best Results

Digital Scale – A digital scale is your best friend when it comes to precise measurements. It ensures that you're using the exact amount of ingredients called for, which is crucial for consistent, perfect results. I highly recommend using a scale when dividing batter or portioning dough to ensure even baking.

Measuring Cups and Spoons – I use metal dry measuring cups for flour and other dry ingredients, and glass measuring cups with spouts for liquids. When it comes to measuring spoons, metal ones are the most reliable for getting accurate measurements.

Bench Scraper – This versatile tool is perfect for lifting dough, transferring ingredients, and cleaning your work surface. It's one of those tools that makes every baking session smoother and more enjoyable.

Offset Spatula – An offset spatula is essential for spreading batter evenly and icing cakes. It gives you more control and helps create a smooth, professional finish on everything from cookies to cupcakes.

Oven Thermometer – Since many ovens can be slightly off in temperature, an oven thermometer ensures that your baked goods are cooked at the correct temperature every time. Just hang it from the center rack of your oven, and you'll always know exactly how hot it is.

Parchment Paper – Parchment paper is a baker's best friend. I use it to line pans for easy removal and to prevent sticking. It's great for cookies, cakes, and even quick breads, making clean-up a breeze.

Pastry Brushes – A natural-bristle pastry brush is great for glazing, coating, and brushing away crumbs. I find that it works much better than silicone brushes, though they need to be replaced more often.

Silicone Spatulas – These are one of the most versatile tools in the kitchen, perfect for stirring, folding, scraping, and mixing. Their flexibility makes them perfect for getting every last bit of batter out of the bowl.

Cooling Racks – Cooling racks are essential for allowing air to circulate around baked goods, helping them cool quickly and ensuring they don't get soggy bottoms. Plus, they help keep your countertops clutter-free while your treats cool.

Zester – A zester is perfect for adding that extra punch of flavor to your baked goods. Whether it's lemon zest in a cake or freshly grated nutmeg in cookies, a good zester can take your desserts to the next level.

1
Mornings' Feast: Breads and Pastries

Cinnamon Rolls

Ingredients

For the Soft Dough Base:
- All-purpose flour: for dusting your work surface
- Fluffy Sweet Dough recipe (chapter 1): about 5/6 of the recipe

Spiced Filling:
- Light brown sugar: 5/12 cup (about 84 g) for a caramel-like sweetness
- Ground cinnamon: 1 generous tablespoon
- Salt: a pinch, to balance the flavors
- Unsalted butter: 1 2/3 tablespoons, melted and cooled for a rich, velvety taste

Creamy and Soft Frosting:
- Butter: 6 2/3 tablespoons (about 94 g), at room temperature for a smooth texture
- Cream cheese: 3 1/3 oz (about 94 g), softened
- Natural vanilla extract: 5/6 teaspoon
- Salt: 1/5 teaspoon, to enhance the flavors
- Confectioners' sugar: 5/6 cup (about 100 g) for a light sweetness 9

Makes 10 Cinnamon Rolls

Directions

1. Prepare the Soft Dough
- On a lightly floured surface, knead the cold dough about 10 times until it's smooth and easier to handle.
- Shape the dough into a ball, lightly dust the top with flour, and cover it with a clean kitchen towel or plastic wrap. Let it rest until it reaches room temperature.
- Meanwhile, generously grease a 9x13-inch (23x33 cm) baking pan, or line it with parchment paper to ensure the cinnamon rolls won't stick.

2. Mix the Sweet-Spiced Filling
- In a small bowl, combine the brown sugar, cinnamon, and a pinch of salt. This warm, fragrant mixture will become the heart of your cinnamon rolls, giving them that classic flavor.
- Lightly flour your work surface again and roll out the dough into a rectangle, about 12x16 inches (30.5x40.5 cm).
- Brush the surface of the dough with the melted butter, covering it evenly. Then sprinkle the cinnamon-sugar mixture over the dough, pressing it gently with your hands to make sure it sticks.
- Starting from one of the long edges, carefully roll up the dough into a tight log. Pinch the seam to seal it, then place the log seam-side down on the counter.
- Using a sharp knife or kitchen scissors, cut the log into 10 equal pieces. Transfer the slices to the prepared baking pan, with the cut side up to show off the beautiful cinnamon swirls.

3. Let the Dough Rise
- Cover the baking pan with plastic wrap and let the dough rise in a warm, draft-free spot until it doubles in size, about 1 to 1.5 hours. This is when the rolls will puff up and become soft and airy.
- While the dough is rising, position a rack in the center of your oven and preheat it to 350°F (180°C).
- Remove the plastic wrap and bake the cinnamon rolls for 27 to 32 minutes, rotating the pan halfway through, until the rolls are lightly golden and fragrant.

4. Make the Creamy Frosting
- While the rolls bake, beat the butter and cream cheese in a stand mixer or with a hand mixer at medium speed until smooth and creamy.

- Add the vanilla extract and salt, mixing on low speed until combined. Gradually add the confectioners' sugar, mixing on low until fully incorporated.
- Scrape down the sides of the bowl, then increase the speed and beat for 3 to 4 minutes until the frosting is light, fluffy, and smooth.

5. Frost the Rolls
- Once baked, transfer the cinnamon rolls to a wire rack and let them cool for about 5 minutes.
- Using an offset spatula or a knife, spread a thin layer of frosting over the warm rolls, allowing it to melt slightly and soak in to enhance their softness.
- Let the rolls cool for another 15 to 20 minutes before applying the remaining frosting. These cinnamon rolls are best enjoyed fresh, warm, and soft, with every bite offering that perfect blend of sweetness and spice.

Tips:
- For Extra Soft Rolls: If you love your cinnamon rolls to be extra soft with a gooey center, spread a thin layer of icing on them immediately after taking them out of the oven. The heat will melt the icing, making every bite more indulgent.

- For a Crispier Texture: If you prefer a slight crunch, allow the rolls to cool completely before adding the icing. This will keep the exterior a bit firmer while maintaining a soft, tender interior.

Filling Variations:

For an even richer filling, spread 5 tablespoons (70 g) of room-temperature unsalted butter evenly across the rolled-out dough. Then, mix together 2/3 cup (135 g) of light brown sugar, 2 tablespoons of ground cinnamon, and a pinch of salt. Sprinkle the mixture over the buttered dough and gently press it down to ensure it sticks well. This will make every bite of your cinnamon rolls even more indulgent and full of flavor.

Cinnamon Rolls with Sugared Cranberries

Prepare the dough as instructed in the main recipe, and roll it out on a lightly floured surface. Spread the classic cinnamon roll filling over the dough, then add a generous dollop of Cranberry Jam (about 1/3 cup or 100g) over the sugar and cinnamon mixture. Roll the dough, cut into pieces, and bake as directed in the main recipe. Once the rolls are frosted, top them with Sugared Cranberries for an extra special touch.

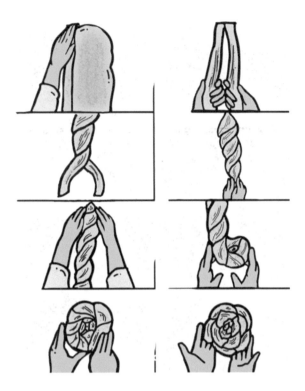

Giant Cinnamon Roll

In a small bowl, combine 1/2 cup (100 g) of light brown sugar, 1 tablespoon of ground cinnamon, and a pinch of salt. Lightly flour your work surface, and roll out half of your Sweet Dough into a 14 by 12-inch (35.5 by 30.5 cm) rectangle.

Brush the dough with 2 tablespoons of melted butter, then evenly sprinkle the cinnamon-sugar mixture over the top, pressing it gently into the butter so it sticks.

Cut the dough into seven equal strips, each about 2 by 12 inches (5 by 30.5 cm). Roll the first strip into a tight spiral. Wrap the second strip around the coil, continuing with each remaining strip until you have a giant cinnamon roll.

Place the dough into a greased and lined 8-inch (20 cm) cake pan. Cover the roll loosely with plastic wrap and let rise until doubled in size, about 1 hour.

Preheat the oven to 350°F (180°C) and bake for 20-28 minutes, until golden brown and set in the center.

Let cool on a wire rack for 5 minutes, then drizzle with icing (as directed in the main recipe), if desired.

Cinnamon Braid

In a small bowl, mix together 1/2 cup (100 g) of light brown sugar, 1 tablespoon of ground cinnamon, and a pinch of salt. Lightly flour your work surface, and roll out half of your Sweet Dough into a 16 by 14-inch (about 40.5 by 35.5 cm) rectangle.

Brush the surface with 2 tablespoons of melted butter, then evenly sprinkle the cinnamon-sugar mixture over the dough, gently pressing it into the butter to help it stick.

Starting from one long side, tightly roll the dough into a cylinder. Pinch the seam to seal it and place the roll seam-side down. Set the roll on a parchment-lined baking sheet, and chill in the refrigerator for 15 minutes.

Using a sharp knife or bench scraper, cut the roll in half lengthwise, then place the halves side by side. Twist them together gently to create a braid. Form the braid into a circle, tucking one end under the braid.

Cover the braid loosely with plastic wrap and let rise for about 1 hour, until it has doubled in size. Preheat your oven to 350°F (180°C), and bake for 20-28 minutes, until golden brown. Once the braid has cooled for about 5 minutes, you can drizzle it with icing, if desired.

22

Nutella Star Bread

Ingredients

- Fluffy Sweet Dough recipe (chapter 1): about half of the recipe
- All-purpose flour: for dusting your work surface
- Chocolate-hazelnut spread or Nutella: 3/4 cup (225 g)
- Egg wash mixture
- Sugar: a bit, for a light sprinkle

Makes 1 loaf

Directions

1. Prepare a baking sheet by lining it with parchment paper. Divide the dough into four equal pieces, roll each into a ball, cover with plastic wrap, and let them rest for 10 minutes.
2. Lightly flour your work surface and roll each ball into a 10-inch (25 cm) circle.
3. Place one circle of dough on the prepared baking sheet. Spread one-third of the Nutella over the top, leaving a 1/2-inch (12 mm) border around the edges. Layer another dough circle on top and repeat with another third of the Nutella. Continue this process, ending with the last dough circle on top, without Nutella.
4. Chill the assembled dough in the refrigerator for 15 minutes to make it easier to work with.
5. Place a 2.5-inch (6 cm) biscuit cutter or glass in the center of the dough stack without pressing down too hard. Using a bench scraper or knife, cut the dough into 16 equal wedges, starting from the edge of the cutter and slicing outward to the edge of the dough.
6. Take two adjacent wedges and twist them away from each other twice, then pinch the ends together to form a star point. Repeat with all the pairs of wedges to complete the star.
7. Remove the biscuit cutter, cover the star with plastic wrap, and let it rise for 45 minutes to 1 hour until the dough is soft and puffy.

8. Preheat the oven to 350°F (180°C). Brush the surface of the star with egg wash and sprinkle sugar over the top for a crispy finish. Bake for 20-28 minutes until the star is golden and aromatic.
9. Let the star cool slightly before serving. This star is best enjoyed fresh from the oven!

Variations

- **Jam-Filled Star**
  Replace the Nutella with your favorite jam for a fruity twist.

- **Cinnamon-Sugar Star**
  For those who love classic cinnamon and sugar, swap the Nutella for the filling used in the Cinnamon Braid.

Morning Buns

Ingredients

- Granulated sugar: 5/6 cup (169 g), plus extra for coating the muffin tin to create a sweet, caramelized crust
- Fresh orange zest: 1 2/3 tablespoons for a burst of citrus brightness
- Ground cinnamon: 2 1/2 teaspoons for cozy warmth
- Salt: a pinch, to balance the flavors
- All-purpose flour: for dusting the work surface
- Easy croissant dough: 1 batch (chapter 1)
- Unsalted butter: 2 1/2 tablespoons, melted, plus extra for generously greasing the muffin tin

Makes 12 buns

Directions

1. Prepare the Muffin Tin: Generously butter the inside and top of a standard 10-cup muffin tin with melted butter. Sprinkle each cup with granulated sugar, tapping out the excess, to give the buns a lovely caramelized crust.
2. Mix the Cinnamon Sugar: In a small bowl, combine 1/2 cup (85 g) of sugar, orange zest, cinnamon, and a pinch of salt. This aromatic blend will bring sweetness and warmth to each bun.
3. Roll Out the Dough: Lightly dust your work surface with flour and roll the croissant dough into a large rectangle, about 10 by 20 inches (25 by 50 cm), keeping the edges as even as possible.
4. Add Butter and Cinnamon Sugar: Brush the surface of the dough with melted butter, then evenly sprinkle the cinnamon-sugar mixture over it, pressing gently to help it stick.
5. Roll and Slice: Starting from one of the long sides, gently roll up the dough into a tight log, keeping the seam side down. Using a sharp knife, cut the roll into 10 equal pieces.
6. Let the Buns Rise: Place each piece in the prepared muffin tin, cut-side up. Cover the muffin tin with plastic wrap and let the buns rise in a warm, draft-free spot until they double in size, about 2 to 2 1/2 hours. For a morning treat, you can also let them rise slowly in the fridge overnight.

- **Baking**

1. Preheat the Oven: Preheat your oven to 400°F (200°C). Remove the plastic wrap and gently press the tops of each bun with a greased spatula to shape them perfectly.
2. Bake the Buns: Place a baking sheet on the lower oven rack to catch any drips. Bake the buns for 15 minutes, then gently press the tops again before baking for an additional 10-15 minutes, until they're golden brown and your kitchen smells heavenly.
3. Coat with Sugar: While the buns are baking, prepare a bowl with the remaining 1/2 cup (85 g) of sugar. Once the buns are out of the oven, immediately turn them out onto a parchment-lined baking sheet. Using tongs, roll each bun in the sugar until well coated.
4. Cool and Enjoy: Let the buns cool slightly on a wire rack, though it's hard to resist tasting them right away! These buns are best enjoyed fresh, warm, and sweet, on the same day they're made.

Overnight Morning Buns:
For a hassle-free morning, prepare the buns as instructed, but instead of letting them rise at room temperature, cover them with plastic wrap and refrigerate for at least 8 hours, or up to 18 hours. In the morning, remove them from the fridge and let them rise at room temperature (still covered) for 1 ½ - 2 hours until puffed and ready to bake.

Variation

Panettone-Inspired Morning Buns: For a festive twist, add 1 tablespoon of lemon zest to the filling, along with 1 cup (169 g) of mixed dried and/or candied fruit. Cranberries, candied orange peel, golden raisins, dried pineapple, apricots, and cherries are all wonderful options. This variation will bring a little holiday cheer to every bite, making each bun a celebration of flavors!

Cranberries and Cream Danish

Ingredients

Cream Cheese Mixture:
- Cream cheese: 4.8 oz (136 g), softened and brought to room temperature
- White sugar: 3.6 tablespoons
- Salt: a dash
- Real vanilla extract: 1 1/4 teaspoons

For Assembling:
- Flour: for dusting the surface
- Easy croissant dough: 0.6 batch
- Egg wash
- Cranberry Sauce with a Holiday Twist (chapter 5)
- White sugar: for a sweet topping

Makes 10 Danish

Directions

- **For the Cream Cheese Filling**

In the bowl of a stand mixer fitted with a paddle attachment, gently beat the cream cheese on medium speed until it's velvety smooth. Add the sugar and a small pinch of salt, then mix again until everything comes together in a creamy, luscious filling. Scrape down the sides of the bowl, add the vanilla, and beat on low speed until fully blended. You can prepare this filling up to two days ahead—it keeps beautifully when stored in an airtight container in the fridge, ready to bring that perfect balance of sweetness to your Danish

- **To Assemble**

1. Prepare two baking sheets by lining them with parchment paper. Lightly dust your work surface with flour, and roll the dough out into a rectangle, about 10 x 18 inches (25 x 46 cm). If needed, use a pastry cutter to tidy up the edges so they're nice and straight, then cut the dough vertically into 10 even strips, each 1 inch wide and 18 inches long. Place the strips on your prepared baking sheets, cover them gently with plastic wrap, and pop them in the fridge for 15 minutes to firm up.

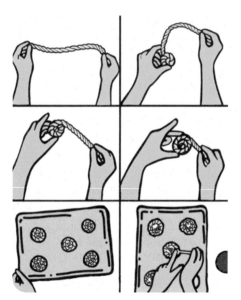

2. Now comes the fun part! Take one end of a dough strip and hold it steady with one hand. With your other hand, gently twist the strip several times, and then curl the twisted dough around itself to create a spiral, tucking the loose end underneath. Continue this process for all the strips, spacing them about 2 inches (5 cm) apart on the baking sheet. Cover them lightly with plastic wrap and let them rest at room temperature for about 2 hours, until the spirals have risen and become soft and puffy—when pressed lightly, they should feel as springy as a marshmallow.

3. While the dough rises, preheat your oven to 400°F (200°C), making sure to position your racks in the upper-middle and lower-middle slots. Right before baking, use your fingertips to gently press a small well into the center of each spiral—this will hold the filling. Brush the tops with a light coating of egg wash, then spoon a teaspoon of cranberry jam and a teaspoon of cream cheese filling into the center of each Danish. Finally, sprinkle the exposed dough with a generous amount of sugar to give it that beautiful sparkle and sweet crunch.

4. Bake for 10 minutes, then rotate the pans and continue baking for another 8 to 10 minutes, until the pastries are perfectly golden. Transfer them to a wire rack to cool, but they're best enjoyed slightly warm, when the flavors are at their peak and the pastry is irresistibly flaky.

Pear-Almond Danish Braid

Ingredients

For the Pear Filling:
- 1 1/2 teaspoons Almond extract:
- 2 large Bartlett pears, peeled and sliced into 1/2-inch [12 mm] pieces
- 1/4 cup [49 g] granulated sugar
- A pinch of salt

For Assembly:
- All-purpose flour
- Danish Dough: 1/2 recipe (chapter 1)
- Egg wash

For the Icing:
- Confectioners' sugar: 3/4 cup [90 g]
- Water: 2 to 4 tablespoons [30 to 59 g]
- Unsalted butter: 1 tablespoon, melted
- Natural vanilla extract: 1/2 teaspoon
- Toasted sliced almonds: 1/2 cup [49 g], for sprinkling

Makes 1 Braid

Directions

- **Making the Pear Filling:**

To start, mix your pear slices with the sugar, almond extract, and a pinch of salt in a small bowl. The delicate fragrance of sweet pears blending with the warmth of almonds is like a promise of something truly delightful. Let this filling sit for a few minutes while you roll out your dough. It's a small moment to pause and appreciate the simplicity of these natural ingredients coming together.

- **To Assemble**

On a lightly floured surface, roll out the dough into a 10 by 14-inch [25 by 35.5 cm] rectangle. Be generous with the flour to prevent any sticking, and remember, there's no rush—enjoy the process. Transfer the dough to a parchment-lined baking sheet, ready for the filling. Spread the pear filling evenly down the middle of the dough, keeping a little space along the edges.

Now, cut 1/2-inch [12 mm] strips along both sides of the dough, keeping the cuts as neat and even as possible. Don't worry if it's not perfect—it's homemade, and that's where the charm lies. Starting at the top, gently cross the strips over each other, creating a lovely braid that wraps the pears in a cozy embrace. Tuck the ends underneath to secure everything in place. Cover the braid with plastic wrap and let it rise until soft and pillowy, about 1 1/2 hours. If you want to make things even easier, you can refrigerate the braid overnight and bake it fresh the next day, allowing the flavors to develop even more.

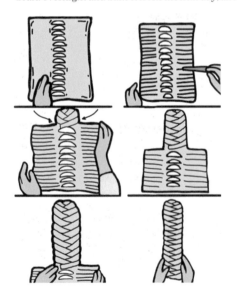

- **Baking the Braid:** Preheat your oven to 350°F (180°C) and brush the braid with egg wash for a golden finish. Bake for 25 to 30 minutes until golden brown and fragrant, then cool slightly on a wire rack.

- **Preparing the Icing:** Whisk together confectioners' sugar, 2 tablespoons of water, melted butter, and vanilla. Adjust the consistency with additional water if needed. Drizzle the icing over the warm braid and sprinkle with toasted almonds for added crunch.

- **Preparing in Advance:** To prep ahead, refrigerate the braid covered with plastic wrap overnight. Allow it to come to room temperature for 1 ½ to 2 hours before baking, then follow the baking instructions and savor your creation while it's fresh and warm.

This braid is more than just a dessert—it's an experience. The joy of making something with your own hands, the pleasure of sharing it with others, and the warmth it brings to your home all add up to something truly special. Enjoy every step of the process, and most of all, savor every bite!

Coffee-Cardamom Bread

Ingredients

For the Dough:

- Whole milk: 1/2 cup (119 g)
- Sour cream: 1/4 cup (59 g)
- Egg: 1 large, plus 2 large egg yolks
- Honey: 2 tablespoons
- Natural vanilla extract: 1 teaspoon
- All-purpose flour: 3 cups plus 1 tablespoon (435 g)
- Granulated sugar: 1/4 cup (49 g)
- Instant yeast: 2 teaspoons
- Salt: 1 1/2 teaspoons
- Unsalted butter: 4 tablespoons (57 g), at room temperature, cut into 1-inch pieces

For the Coating:

- Unsalted butter: 6 tablespoons (84 g), melted
- Granulated sugar: 3/4 cup (149 g)
- Ground cardamom: 1 teaspoon
- Fine sea salt: 1/4 teaspoon

For the Coffee Caramel:

- Strong, freshly brewed coffee: 1/2 cup (119 g)
- Corn syrup: 3 tablespoons
- Unsalted butter: 8 tablespoons (1 stick or 114 g)
- Light brown sugar: 3/4 cup (149 g)
- Granulated sugar: 1/4 cup (49 g)
- Salt: 1/2 teaspoon
- Kahlúa: 1 tablespoon (optional)

Makes one 10 in (25 cm) bundt

Directions

- **For the dough**

1. In a large bowl or liquid measuring cup, mix together the milk, sour cream, egg, yolks, honey, and vanilla. Make sure all the ingredients are at room temperature for a smooth, even dough.
2. In the bowl of a stand mixer fitted with a dough hook, combine the flour, granulated sugar, yeast, and salt. Mix on low speed until the dry ingredients are well incorporated.
3. Slowly pour in the liquid mixture while the mixer is running on low. At first, the dough will look a bit rough, but don't worry— it will come together as it kneads.
4. Increase the mixer speed to medium and knead for 6 to 8 minutes, until the dough is elastic and smooth. If needed, scrape down the sides of the bowl to make sure everything is well mixed.
5. Add the butter, one piece at a time, and continue mixing on low speed until fully incorporated. The butter gives the dough its soft, rich texture. If the dough seems too sticky, add a tablespoon of flour at a time, but be careful not to overdo it—the dough should remain soft.
6. Transfer the dough to a lightly greased bowl, cover with plastic wrap, and let it rise in a warm, draft-free place until it has doubled in size. This should take about 1 1/2 to 2 hours, depending on the temperature of your kitchen.

- **For the coating**

1. Melt the butter in a small saucepan or in the microwave and pour it into a large bowl.
2. In a separate bowl, whisk together the sugar, cardamom, and salt. This fragrant mixture will give the monkey bread its irresistible flavor.
3. Once the dough has risen, divide it into small balls about 1 1/2 inches in size. Dip each ball in the melted butter, making sure they are well coated.
4. Roll the buttered dough balls in the sugar-cardamom mixture, pressing lightly to ensure they are thoroughly covered.
5. Arrange the dough balls in a well-greased Bundt pan, placing them snugly together. They will puff up during baking to create a beautiful, layered effect.

- **For the coffee caramel**

1. While the dough is resting, prepare the caramel. In a medium saucepan, combine the coffee, corn syrup, butter, brown sugar, granulated sugar, and salt.
2. Bring the mixture to a boil over medium heat, stirring frequently to prevent the sugars from sticking to the bottom of the pan. Let it simmer for 6 to 8 minutes until the caramel thickens slightly and becomes glossy.
3. For an extra layer of flavor, stir in the Kahlúa, if using. Once ready, pour the caramel evenly over the dough balls in the Bundt pan. The caramel will seep through the layers, making each bite deliciously sticky and sweet.

- **Baking**
- 1. Preheat the oven to 350°F (180°C). Place a baking sheet underneath the Bundt pan to catch any drips of caramel.
- 2. Bake the monkey bread for 35 to 40 minutes, or until the top is golden and the caramel is bubbling. If using a Pullman loaf pan, the baking time may increase slightly to 42 to 45 minutes.
- 3. Let the monkey bread cool in the pan for 8 to 10 minutes before carefully inverting it onto a serving platter. The rich aroma of coffee and caramel will fill your kitchen, creating a warm, inviting atmosphere.
- 4. Serve the monkey bread warm, pulling apart each soft, sticky piece. It's best enjoyed fresh from the oven, but leftovers can be gently reheated if needed.

For an overnight version:
After assembling the monkey bread, cover it with plastic wrap and refrigerate for 8 to 18 hours. When ready to bake, let it sit at room temperature for 45 to 60 minutes before placing it in the oven.

Cinnamon Sugar Monkey Bread Variation:
For a more traditional flavor, omit the cardamom from the coating and replace it with 1 tablespoon of ground cinnamon. You can also leave out the coffee and Kahlúa from the caramel for a simpler, sweeter version.

This heartwarming recipe is perfect for a special breakfast or holiday treat, bringing people together around the table to share not just food, but moments of sweetness and joy.

Powdered Sugar Donuts

Ingredients

For the Donuts:
- Whole milk: 1/2 cup [119 g]
- Sour cream: 1/4 cup [59 g]
- Egg: 1 large, plus 2 large egg yolks, at room temperature
- Honey: 2 tablespoons
- Natural vanilla extract: 1 tablespoon
- All-purpose flour: 3 cups [426 g], plus extra for dusting
- Granulated sugar: 1/4 cup [49 g]
- Instant dry yeast: 1 tablespoon
- Salt: 1 1/2 teaspoons
- Unsalted butter: 8 tablespoons [1 stick or 114 g], at room temperature, cut into 1-inch [2.5 cm] pieces

For the Sugar Coating:
- Confectioners' sugar: 1 cup [119 g]
- Ground nutmeg: 1 1/2 teaspoons

For Assembly:
- Canola oil: enough to fill a medium to large Dutch oven about 4 inches [10 cm] deep, for frying
- Unsalted butter: 3 tablespoons, melted

Makes 2 dozen mini donut

Directions

- **For the Donuts:**

1. In a medium bowl or liquid measuring cup, whisk together the milk, sour cream, egg, yolks, honey, and vanilla. Set aside. In the bowl of a stand mixer fitted with a dough hook, mix together the flour, sugar, yeast, and salt on low speed. Slowly add the wet ingredients to the dry, continuing to mix on low until combined. The dough will look shaggy at first, but as you knead it on medium speed for about 6 to 8 minutes, it will become smooth and elastic. Make sure to scrape down the sides of the bowl as needed.

2. Once the dough pulls away from the sides of the bowl, start adding the butter one piece at a time, mixing on low speed until each piece is fully incorporated. This process will take a few minutes, but don't rush—let the butter work its way into the dough. Increase the speed to medium-low and knead for 2 to 3 more minutes, until the dough is completely smooth. If the dough is sticking to the bowl, sprinkle in an additional tablespoon of flour and continue kneading.

3. Transfer the dough to a large, greased bowl. Cover it with plastic wrap and let it rise in a warm, draft-free spot until it has doubled in size, about 1½ to 2 hours. You can refrigerate the dough at this point for up to overnight if you'd like.

4. Once the dough is ready, transfer it to a lightly floured work surface. Cut out 24 small pieces of parchment paper, and using a 2-inch [5 cm] biscuit cutter, cut the dough into small rounds. You can use a smaller cutter to remove the center of each round to create the donut shape. Place two donuts on each piece of parchment paper and arrange them on two sheet pans, spacing them out so they have room to rise. Cover the donuts with greased plastic wrap and let them rise again for about 1½ hours, or until almost doubled in size.

- **For the Sugar Coating:**

In a medium bowl, whisk together the confectioners' sugar and ground nutmeg until fully combined.

- **To Assemble:**

1. Heat the oil in a large Dutch oven, wok, or deep fryer to 365°F [185°C]. Carefully place two donuts (with the parchment paper) into a wire basket or spider skimmer, and gently drop them into the hot oil. Fry the donuts for about 1 minute on each side, until golden brown and fully cooked. Remove the parchment paper as the donuts fry.

2. Use the skimmer to transfer the donuts to a wire rack lined with paper towels, allowing them to cool for 1 to 2 minutes before brushing them with melted butter. Then, toss the warm donuts in the prepared sugar coating, making sure each donut is fully covered. For an extra touch, sift more powdered sugar over the top of the donuts just before serving. These donuts are best enjoyed right away while they're still warm.

- **Make It Early: For Overnight Donuts**

To make the donuts ahead, cut the dough into rounds as directed and refrigerate them overnight instead of letting them rise for 1½ hours. When you're ready to fry, allow the donuts to come to room temperature for 1 to 1½ hours before frying. Fry as directed above.

Coffee Cake with Streusel Topping

Ingredients

For the Coffee Cake:
- Whole milk: 1 cup (240 g), at room temperature
- Large egg whites: 1 scant cup (211 g), about 6 or 7 eggs, at room temperature
- Homemade French Crème Fraîche (chapter 5) or sour cream: 1/2 cup (119 g), at room temperature
- Natural vanilla extract: 1 tablespoon
- All-purpose flour: 2 3/4 cups (391 g)
- Granulated sugar: 2 cups (399 g)
- Baking powder: 4 teaspoons
- Salt: 1 teaspoon
- Unsalted butter: 1 cup (227 g), at room temperature, cut into 1-inch (2.5 cm) pieces

For Cream Cheese Filling:
- Cream cheese: 4 oz (114 g), at room temperature
- Granulated sugar: 2 tablespoons
- Cozy Crumble Topping (chapter 5): 1 1/2 cups (188 g)

For Icing Ingredients:
- Confectioners' sugar: 1 1/2 cups (179 g)
- Water: 2 to 4 tablespoons (30 to 59 g)
- Butter: 1 tablespoon, melted
- Natural vanilla extract: 1/2 teaspoon

Makes 12 large or 16 small servings

Directions

- **For the Coffee Cake:**
1. Prepare the batter: In a medium bowl, whisk together the milk, egg whites, crème fraîche, and vanilla. In the bowl of a stand mixer fitted with a paddle attachment, combine the flour, granulated sugar, baking powder, and salt. With the mixer on low speed, gradually add the butter, mixing until the mixture resembles coarse crumbs.
2. Mix the wet and dry ingredients: Slowly pour in half of the wet ingredients while the mixer runs. Increase the speed to medium and beat until everything is well combined, about 30 seconds. Lower the speed and add the remaining wet ingredients, mixing until just combined. Then, turn up the mixer again for another 20 seconds to smooth out the batter, scraping the bowl as needed to make sure everything is well incorporated.
3. Pour into the pan: Grease a 9x13 inch (23x33 cm) pan and line it with parchment paper. Pour the batter into the prepared pan, setting aside just a tablespoon of the batter for the cream cheese filling.

- **Making the Cream Cheese Filling:**
1. In a small bowl, mix together the cream cheese and sugar until smooth. Stir in the tablespoon of reserved cake batter until everything is creamy and well blended.
2. Swirl in the filling: Spoon the cream cheese filling over the cake batter in the pan and gently swirl it with a knife to create beautiful, delicate patterns.
3. Top with streusel: Sprinkle the streusel topping evenly across the cake, ensuring that every bite will have a delightful crunch.

- **Baking the Cake:**
1. Preheat your oven to 350°F (180°C). Bake the cake for 28 to 35 minutes, turning the pan halfway through baking to ensure even browning. The cake is done when it turns a lovely golden brown and a toothpick inserted in the center comes out with a few moist crumbs.
2. Let it cool: Once the cake is done, let it cool in the pan for about 5 minutes, then transfer it to a wire rack to cool completely.

- **Prepare the Icing:**
1. While the cake is baking, mix together the confectioners' sugar, water (start with 2 tablespoons), melted butter, and vanilla in a medium bowl. Stir until smooth, adding more water a tablespoon at a time if needed to get the desired consistency.
2. Glaze the cake: Pour half the icing over the warm cake, allowing it to settle into the nooks and crannies. Let the cake sit for 20 minutes, then pour the remaining icing on top for a finishing touch of sweetness.

Variation

For a refreshing twist, try the lemon version of this cake! Instead of the cream cheese filling, swirl 3/4 cup (240 g) of lemon curd into the batter before adding the streusel topping. For the icing, replace the water with fresh lemon juice for a bright and zesty flavor.

Panettone Scones

Ingredients

- Granulated sugar: 1/3 cup (65 g), plus extra for sprinkling
- Orange zest: 1 tablespoon
- All-purpose flour: 2 1/4 cups (320 g), plus more as needed
- Baking powder: 1 tablespoon
- Salt: 1/2 teaspoon
- Homemade French Crème Fraîche (chapter 5) or sour cream: 1/2 cup (119 g)
- Heavy cream: 1/4 cup (59 g), plus extra for brushing
- Egg: 1 large, plus 1 large egg yolk
- Natural vanilla extract: 1 teaspoon
- Unsalted butter: 12 tablespoons (169 g), cut into 1/2-inch pieces
- Dried fruit (cherries, apricots, Sugary Citrus Peel Delights (chapter 5) candied ginger, cranberries, or pineapple): 1/2 cup (70 g)
- Almond paste: 8 oz (226 g)

Makes 8 scones

Directions

1. **Preheat the oven:** Adjust the oven rack to the middle position and preheat the oven to 400°F (200°C). Stack two baking sheets on top of each other and line the top sheet with parchment paper. This helps prevent the bottoms from browning too quickly.
2. **Prepare the dry ingredients:** In a large bowl, use your hands to rub the orange zest into the sugar until fragrant. This step brings out the oils in the zest, infusing the sugar with citrusy goodness. Add the flour, baking powder, and salt. Whisk everything together until well combined.
3. **Mix the wet ingredients:** In a medium bowl or liquid measuring cup, whisk together the crème fraîche, heavy cream, egg, egg yolk, and vanilla. Set aside.
4. **Incorporate the butter:** Add the cold butter pieces to the dry ingredients. Use a pastry cutter or your fingertips to cut the butter into the flour mixture until it resembles small peas. You want the butter to stay cold so it melts while baking, creating flaky layers.
5. **Combine wet and dry:** Slowly add the wet ingredients to the dry, gently folding with a spatula until just combined. Be careful not to overmix. Gently fold in the dried fruit, distributing it evenly throughout the dough.
6. **Shape the dough:** Transfer the dough to a lightly floured surface and knead it four to six times, just until it comes together. Pat the dough into a 12-inch (30.5 cm) square, dusting with flour as needed to prevent sticking. Fold the dough into thirds like a letter, then fold the short ends into thirds again to form a square. Chill the dough in the freezer for 10 minutes.
7. **Prepare the almond paste:** While the dough is chilling, roll the almond paste into a 12-inch (30.5 cm) square. Once the dough is chilled, roll it out again to 12 inches and place the almond paste on top. Fold the dough over the almond paste into thirds, then chill for another 10 minutes.
8. **Cut the scones:** Roll the dough out to a 12 x 4-inch (30.5 x 10 cm) rectangle. Cut the dough crosswise into four equal rectangles, then cut each rectangle diagonally to create triangles. Brush the tops with heavy cream and sprinkle generously with sugar.
9. **Bake:** Place the scones on the prepared baking sheet and bake for 18 to 25 minutes, rotating the pan halfway through. Bake until the tops are golden brown and crisp. Let the scones cool on a wire rack for about 10 minutes before serving. They're best enjoyed fresh out of the oven!

Variation

Once the unbaked scones are cut into triangles, freeze them in a single layer on a sheet pan. Once frozen solid, transfer them to a freezer-safe bag and store for up to two weeks. Bake directly from frozen, adding a few extra minutes to the bake time.

Easy croissant dough

Ingredients

- Warm water (100°F to 110°F [35°C to 45°C]): 1 1/2 cups (359 g)
- Active dry yeast: 4 teaspoons
- All-purpose flour: 4 cups plus 1 tablespoon (577 g), plus more for dusting
- Granulated sugar: 1/4 cup plus 1 tablespoon (63 g)
- Salt: 2 teaspoons

- Unsalted butter: 2 tablespoons, melted
- Unsalted European butter (preferably 83-84% butterfat), at room temperature (68°F [20°C]): 1 1/2 cups (339 g)

Makes about 2 1/2 lb (1.2 kg) of Dough

Directions

1. **Activate the Yeast:** In a small bowl or liquid measuring cup, mix the warm water and yeast. Let it sit for about 5 minutes until the yeast dissolves and starts to foam.
2. **Prepare the Dough:** In the bowl of a stand mixer fitted with a dough hook, combine 4 cups (568 g) of the flour, sugar, and salt. With the mixer on low speed, slowly add the yeast mixture followed by the melted butter. Mix until all the ingredients are combined and the dough starts to come together, about 3 to 4 minutes.

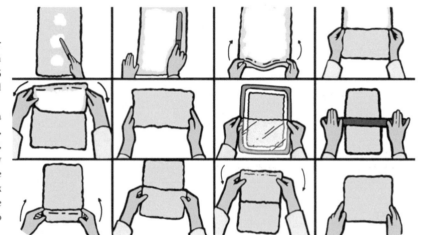

The dough will be rough and bumpy at this stage.

3. **Let the Dough Rise:** Place the dough in a greased bowl, cover with plastic wrap, and let it rise at room temperature for 1 1/2 to 2 hours until it doubles in size.
4. **Prepare for Rolling:** After rising, press the dough down gently to release some gas. Shape it into a 10 x 12-inch (25 x 30.5 cm) rectangle on plastic wrap, wrap it fully, and place on a sheet pan. Refrigerate for at least 2 hours, or overnight.
5. **Prepare the Butter:** In a stand mixer with a paddle attachment, beat the European butter and 1 tablespoon of flour until smooth, creamy, and spreadable, about 2-3 minutes.
6. **Roll and Fold:** Roll the chilled dough on a floured surface into a 12 x 20-inch (30.5 x 50 cm) rectangle. Spread the butter evenly, leaving a 1/2 inch (12 mm) border around the edges.
7. **First Letter Fold:** Fold one-third of the dough over itself, then the other third on top. Rotate the dough so the seam faces right and open ends face you. Roll into a 10 x 18-inch (25 x 46 cm) rectangle.
8. **Chill and Fold Again:** Place the dough on a sheet pan and chill for 6 minutes. Remove and fold again, rolling into an 8 x 16-inch (20 x 40.5 cm) rectangle. Repeat one more letter fold.
9. **Final Chill:** After the last fold, gently compress the dough with a rolling pin. For immediate use, chill the dough for 6 minutes. Alternatively, wrap in plastic and freeze for up to 2 weeks. If frozen, thaw overnight in the refrigerator before use.

- Avoid overmixing the dough to prevent a tough, chewy texture.
- The butter-flour mixture should be creamy and spreadable (like cream cheese) to allow even spreading without tearing the dough
- After chilling, remove the dough from the freezer promptly after 6 minutes. If it gets too hard, let it rest at room temperature until it's pliable enough to roll smoothly.

Danish Dough

Ingredients

- Warm whole milk (100°F to 110°F [35°C to 45°C]): 3/4 cup (179 g)
- Egg: 1 large, plus 2 large egg yolks, at room temperature
- Granulated sugar: 2 tablespoons
- Instant yeast: 2 1/4 teaspoons
- Salt: 1 teaspoon
- Ground cardamom: 1 teaspoon (optional, but so comforting!)
- Unsalted butter: 4 tablespoons (57 g), at room temperature
- Natural vanilla extract: 1 teaspoon
- All-purpose flour: 2 1/2 cups (355 g), plus more for dusting
- Unsalted butter: 12 tablespoons (1 1/2 sticks or 169 g), cold, cut into 24 pieces, plus more for greasing the bowl

Makes 12 buns

Directions

1. **Prepare the Wet Ingredients:** In a large liquid measuring cup, whisk together the warm milk, egg, yolks, and vanilla until everything is beautifully blended. Set this aside. This mixture will give your dough a rich, golden color and a soft, pillowy texture.
2. **Prepare the Dry Ingredients:** In the bowl of a stand mixer fitted with the paddle attachment, combine the flour, sugar, yeast, salt, and cardamom (if using). The cardamom adds such a warm, comforting note to the dough. With the mixer on low speed, gradually add the room-temperature butter and mix until it's fully incorporated into the flour mixture, with no visible pieces of butter remaining.
3. **Mix in the Cold Butter:** Add the cold butter pieces and continue mixing on low speed. You want the butter to be broken down, but not completely. There should still be small, visible bits of butter throughout the dough—this is what helps create those lovely layers. When the butter is about the size of peas, it's time to move on to the next step.
4. **Mix the Wet and Dry Ingredients:** With the mixer still on low, slowly pour in the milk mixture. Keep mixing until the dough starts to come together. It will be quite sticky, with visible lumps of butter—don't worry, this is exactly how it should be! Using a spatula, transfer the dough into a greased bowl, cover it tightly with plastic wrap, and let it rest in the refrigerator overnight, or for up to 3 days. This rest time allows the dough to develop a deeper flavor and makes it easier to work with.
5. **Prepare to Roll:** The next day, when you're ready to work with the dough, transfer it to a well-floured work surface. Knead the dough gently 10 to 12 times, just enough to bring it together into a smooth ball. Lightly dust the top of the dough with flour, cover it with a tea towel, and let it rest at room temperature for a few minutes.
6. **Rolling and Folding:** Pat the dough into a 6-inch (15 cm) square, and then roll it out into a larger rectangle, about 16 by 20 inches (40.5 by 50 cm). If the dough sticks at all, don't be shy about dusting it with more flour. You want to create a nice, even surface to work with. Brush off any excess flour with a pastry brush before folding.
7. **First Turn (Folding the Dough):** Using a bench scraper, fold the dough into thirds like you would fold a letter. This is the first "turn" that will help create the layers. Rotate the dough 90 degrees, and roll it out again to a smaller rectangle, about 8 by 16 inches (20 by 40.5 cm). Repeat the folding process to create multiple layers in the dough.
8. **Repeat and Rest:** Perform a total of four turns, resting the dough in between as needed. On the final turn, gently roll the dough to compress the layers slightly, then wrap it tightly in plastic wrap. Chill the dough for at least 1 hour before using, or keep it in the refrigerator for up to 2 days.
9. **Freezing for Later:** If you're not using the dough right away, you can freeze it for up to 2 weeks. After the final fold, divide the dough into portions, wrap them tightly in plastic wrap, and place in a freezer-safe bag. Thaw the dough in the refrigerator overnight before using.

This Danish dough is so versatile and forgiving, making it perfect for both beginners and seasoned bakers. It's a beautiful base for everything from fruit-filled pastries to savory bites, and once you get the hang of it, you'll find yourself reaching for this recipe time and time again.

Fluffy Sweet Dough

Ingredients

- Eggs: 4 large, at room temperature
- Warm whole milk (100°F to 110°F [35°C to 45°C]): 3/4 cup (179 g)
- Honey: 1/4 cup (85 g)
- All-purpose flour: 4 cups (568 g)
- Instant yeast: 2 1/4 teaspoons (see notes)
- Salt: 2 teaspoons
- Unsalted butter: 10 tablespoons (1 1/4 sticks or 142 g), at room temperature, cut into 1-inch (2.5 cm) pieces, plus more for greasing the bowl

MakeAbout 2 1/2 lbs (1.2 kg) of dough

Directions

1. **Preparing the Dough:** Begin by greasing a large mixing bowl with butter, giving your dough a comfortable home to rest and rise. In a large liquid measuring cup, whisk together the eggs, warm milk, and honey, creating a rich and sweet base for your dough.
2. **Mixing the Dry Ingredients:** In the bowl of a stand mixer fitted with a paddle attachment, combine the flour, instant yeast, and salt on low speed. This is the beginning of the magic. Slowly pour in the egg mixture, allowing the dough to come together bit by bit. Continue mixing until combined.
3. **Adding the Butter:** With the mixer still running on low, add the room-temperature butter one piece at a time, letting each piece melt into the dough before adding the next. Once all the butter is incorporated, increase the speed to medium, beating for 1 minute until smooth. The dough will be sticky, but that's just how it should be!
4. **First Rise:** Scrape the dough into the prepared bowl, cover it tightly with plastic wrap, and let it rise for 30 minutes. This is where the dough starts to grow, puffing up with promise.
5. **Folding the Dough:** Now, here's the gentle part—using your fingers, carefully lift the dough from underneath, pulling it up and over itself. Rotate the bowl slightly and repeat, folding the dough six to eight times in total. This helps strengthen the structure of the dough without overworking it. Re-cover the bowl with plastic wrap and let the dough rise for another 30 minutes.
6. **Repeating the Folding:** Repeat the folding process three more times, every 30 minutes, for a total of four folds. After the final fold, the dough will be soft, elastic, and ready for its long rest. Cover the bowl tightly with plastic wrap and refrigerate overnight, or for up to 72 hours, allowing the flavors to develop and the dough to become even more tender.

Notes:

- **Using Active Yeast:** If you don't have instant yeast, you can substitute active dry yeast. The only difference is that active yeast has larger granules, so dissolve it in the warm milk mixture before adding it to the flour.
- **Chilling the Dough:** Be sure to chill the dough after folding—this makes it much easier to roll out. Without chilling, the dough will be too sticky to handle.

This dough is a beautiful starting point for countless baked goods, offering a soft, buttery, and deliciously tender base for your favorite treats.

Take your time with it, and enjoy the simple pleasure of crafting something so special with your own hands.

2
Festive Sweets and Treats

White Cake with Cranberries and White Chocolate Buttercream

Ingredients

- Whole milk: 1 cup (240 g), at room temperature
- Large egg whites: 1 scant cup (211 g), from 6 or 7 eggs, at room temperature
- Homemade French Crème Fraîche (chapter 5) or sour cream: 1/2 cup (119 g), at room temperature
- Natural vanilla extract: 1 tablespoon
- All-purpose flour: 2 3/4 cups (391 g)
- Granulated sugar: 2 cups (399 g)
- Baking powder: 4 teaspoons
- Salt: 1 teaspoon
- Unsalted butter: 1 cup (227 g), at room temperature, cut into 1-inch (2.5 cm) pieces

For the White Chocolate Buttercream:

- White chocolate: 8 oz (226 g), good quality, chopped
- Unsalted butter: 1 1/2 cups (339 g), at room temperature
- Light corn syrup: 3 tablespoons
- Salt: a pinch
- Confectioners' sugar: 2 cups (240 g)
- Heavy cream: 2 tablespoons
- Natural vanilla extract: 1 tablespoon

For Sugared Cranberries:

- Water: 3/4 cup (179 g)
- Granulated sugar: 1 1/4 cups (249 g), divided
- Salt: a pinch
- Fresh cranberries: 6 oz (169 g)

Assembly:

- Cranberry Sauce with a Holiday Twist (chapter 5)

Makes 8 to 10 servings

Directions

For the Cake

1. Preheat your oven to 350°F (180°C). Butter and flour three 8-by-2-inch (20-by-5 cm) round cake pans and line the bottoms with parchment paper. In a medium bowl or liquid measuring cup, whisk together the milk, egg whites, crème fraîche, and vanilla.

2. In the bowl of a stand mixer fitted with a paddle attachment, combine the flour, sugar, baking powder, and salt. With the mixer on low speed, add the butter one piece at a time until the mixture resembles coarse sand. Gradually add a little more than half of the wet ingredients while mixing on low speed. Once incorporated, turn up the speed to medium and beat for about 30 seconds until smooth.

3. Add the rest of the wet ingredients and continue mixing on low speed until just combined. Increase the speed to medium and mix for another 20 seconds. Scrape down the sides and bottom of the bowl and mix for a few more seconds until everything is well incorporated.

4. Divide the batter evenly between the prepared cake pans, smoothing the tops with a spatula. Tap the pans on the counter to release any air bubbles. Bake for 28 to 35 minutes, rotating the pans halfway through. The cakes should be golden brown, and a toothpick inserted into the center should come out with a few moist crumbs. Let the cakes cool in the pans for 30 minutes before transferring to a wire rack to cool completely.

For the Buttercream

1. While the cakes are baking, heat about 1 inch (2.5 cm) of water in a medium saucepan to a gentle simmer. Melt the white chocolate in a heatproof bowl over the simmering water, stirring constantly until smooth, being careful not to overheat it. Remove from heat and let the chocolate cool slightly.

2. In the bowl of a stand mixer, beat the butter on medium speed until light and creamy, about 3 minutes. Add the corn syrup and salt, mixing until combined.

3. Gradually add the confectioners' sugar and beat on medium speed until fluffy and creamy, scraping the sides as needed, about 2 to 3 minutes. Slowly add the cooled white chocolate, mixing on low speed until completely incorporated.

4. Finish by adding the heavy cream and vanilla, beating until smooth.

For the Sugared Cranberries

In a small saucepan, combine the water, 3/4 cup (149 g) of the sugar, and the salt over medium heat. Stir until the sugar dissolves and bring the mixture to a simmer. Reduce the heat and add the cranberries. Stir gently and cook for 5 to 7 minutes until the cranberries are just softened. Pour the cranberries and syrup into a medium container and refrigerate for at least 8 hours (or up to 24 hours). Once soaked, drain the cranberries and roll them in the remaining 1/2 cup (100 g) of sugar to coat. Let them dry on a parchment-lined baking sheet for a few hours before using.

To Assemble

Place one cake layer on a serving plate or cake stand. Spread 3 tablespoons of cranberry jam evenly across the top. Add the second cake layer and repeat, spreading another 3 tablespoons of jam. Finally, place the third cake layer on top and coat the entire cake with the buttercream. Decorate with sugared cranberries. The cake can be stored in the fridge for up to 24 hours. Before serving, bring it to room temperature to ensure all the flavors shine.

Note:

If using store-bought egg whites, make sure they are 100 percent liquid egg whites, as they won't be whipped for volume in this recipe.

Carrot Cake with Caramelized Honey Buttercream

Ingredients

- Large egg whites: 1 scant cup [211 g], from 6 or 7 large eggs, at room temperature
- Whole milk: 1 cup [240 g], at room temperature
- Canola oil: 1/4 cup [59 g]
- Sour cream: 2 tablespoons, at room temperature
- Natural vanilla extract: 1 teaspoon
- All-purpose flour: 3 cups [426 g]
- Granulated sugar: 1 cup [199 g]
- Light brown sugar: 1 cup [199 g]
- Baking powder: 4 teaspoons
- Ground cinnamon: 2 teaspoons
- Salt: 1 teaspoon
- Cloves: a pinch

- Unsalted butter: 12 tablespoons [1 1/2 sticks or 169 g], at room temperature, cut into 1-inch [2.5 cm] pieces
- Finely grated carrots: 4 cups [399 g]

Burnt Honey Buttercream:

- Large egg whites: 1 cup plus 2 tablespoons [279 g], from 7 or 8 large eggs, at room temperature
- Cream of tartar: 1/4 teaspoon
- Granulated sugar: 1 1/2 cups [300 g]
- Honey: 1/2 cup [169 g]
- Salt: 1/4 teaspoon
- Water: 1/4 cup [59 g]
- Unsalted butter: 3 cups [6 sticks or 678 g], at room temperature, cut into 1-inch [2.5 cm] pieces
- Natural vanilla extract: 1 teaspoon

Assembly:

- Sugared & Spiced Candied Nuts (pecan variation, chapter 5): for decorating (optional)

Makes 8 to 12 servings

Directions

For the Cake

1. Preheat your oven to 350°F [180°C], adjusting an oven rack to the middle position. Grease three 8 by 2 in [20 by 5 cm] round cake pans and line the bottoms with parchment paper. The key to a perfectly baked cake is taking the time to prepare the pans properly, ensuring that the cakes will release without a hitch once they've cooled.
2. In a medium bowl, whisk together the egg whites, milk, oil, sour cream, and vanilla. The combination of these ingredients brings both moisture and richness to the cake.
3. In the bowl of a stand mixer fitted with a paddle, whisk together the flour, granulated and brown sugars, baking powder, cinnamon, salt, and cloves. The warmth of these spices will fill your kitchen as the cake bakes, setting the stage for the cozy treat ahead.
4. With the mixer on low speed, add the butter one piece at a time, blending until the mixture resembles coarse sand. This method ensures that the butter is evenly incorporated, creating a tender crumb.
5. Slowly pour in more than half of the wet ingredients with the mixer running, then increase the speed to medium, beating until the ingredients are well combined, about 30 seconds.
6. Lower the mixer speed and add the remaining wet ingredients, mixing just until combined. Then increase the speed to medium and beat for 20 seconds to smooth out the batter.
7. Use a spatula to fold in the grated carrots, ensuring they are evenly distributed throughout the batter.
8. Divide the batter evenly between the prepared pans and smooth the tops. Tap the pans gently on the counter a few times to eliminate any air bubbles. Bake the cakes for 30 to 36 minutes, rotating the pans halfway through. The kitchen will soon be filled with the sweet, spiced aroma of baking cake.
9. Once a toothpick inserted in the center comes out clean, the cakes are ready. Let them cool in the pans for 30 minutes before transferring them to a wire rack to cool completely.

For the Buttercream

1. In the bowl of a stand mixer, beat the egg whites and cream of tartar on medium speed until soft peaks form, about 5 to 7 minutes. Watching the egg whites transform is like witnessing magic—it goes from liquid to fluffy peaks, waiting to become the perfect buttercream.
2. Slowly add 1/2 cup [100 g] of granulated sugar in a gentle stream while the mixer is running on low speed, then beat until the whites are stiff and glossy, about 1 to 2 minutes.

3. In a medium saucepan, combine the remaining 1 cup [199 g] granulated sugar, honey, and salt. Pour the water over the mixture and stir gently to wet the sugar.
4. Heat over medium heat, occasionally swirling the pan, until the sugar is melted and the mixture looks clear. Increase the heat and let the mixture bubble until it turns a deep golden brown, 3 to 4 minutes.
5. Slowly pour about 2 tablespoons of the hot caramel into the egg whites, mixing constantly to temper the eggs. Continue pouring the caramel in a steady stream while the mixer runs on low speed, then beat until combined.
6. Increase the speed to medium-high and whisk until the bowl cools to room temperature. Lower the speed and add the butter one piece at a time, beating well after each addition.
7. Increase the speed and whisk the buttercream until smooth and creamy. Finally, mix in the vanilla and beat for 1 to 2 minutes until fully incorporated. This buttercream is unlike any other, with its deep, caramel notes perfectly balancing the sweetness of the cake.

To Assemble

1. Place one cake layer on a turntable or serving plate, and with an offset spatula, spread the top evenly with 1 1/2 cups [449 g] of the buttercream. Repeat with the second layer, frosting with another 1 cup [300 g] of buttercream.
2. Top with the third layer and frost the cake all over, smoothing the sides and top for a beautiful finish. If desired, decorate with candied pecans for added crunch.
3. The cake can be stored in the refrigerator for up to 1 day. Bring it to room temperature before serving so that every slice is as soft and tender as possible.

Notes:
- If you're craving a bit more spice, feel free to add 3/4 teaspoon of ginger and 1/4 teaspoon of nutmeg along with the cinnamon.
- If you prefer cream cheese frosting, you can swap out the buttercream for the frosting from the Sprinkle Celebration Cake (chapter 4). It pairs just as wonderfully with this carrot cake!

This cake is like a warm embrace in dessert form. Each bite is filled with tender, spiced cake and smooth, caramel-like buttercream. It's the kind of cake that brings people together, perfect for sharing and making memories.

Layered Chocolate Mousse Delight (Triple Chocolate Mousse Cake)

Ingredients

For the Crust:
- Chocolate wafer cookies: 1 1/2 cups [149 g]
- Unsalted butter: 3 tablespoons, melted

For the Cake:
- Semisweet or bittersweet chocolate: 6 oz [169 g]
- Unsalted butter: 8 tablespoons [1 stick or 114 g]
- Dutch-process cocoa powder: 2 tablespoons
- Granulated sugar: 1 cup [199 g]
- Eggs: 4 large, at room temperature
- Natural vanilla extract: 1 teaspoon
- Salt: 1/4 teaspoon
- All-purpose flour: 1/4 cup [36 g]

For the Chocolate Mousse:
- Heavy cream: 1 3/4 cups [420 g]
- Egg yolks: 5 large, at room temperature
- Granulated sugar: 1/4 cup [49 g]
- Salt: 1/4 teaspoon
- Natural vanilla extract: 1 teaspoon
- Semisweet or bittersweet chocolate: 8 oz [226 g], finely chopped

For the Chocolate Ganache:
- Semisweet or bittersweet chocolate: 6 oz [169 g]
- Heavy cream: 1/2 cup [119 g]
- Cocoa powder

Makes 8 to 12 servings

Directions

For the Crust:
1. Preheat your oven to 350°F [180°C] and adjust an oven rack to the middle position.
2. Grease a 9-inch [23 cm] springform pan.
3. Using a food processor, blend the chocolate wafer cookies into fine crumbs. Transfer the crumbs to a medium bowl and stir in the melted butter until combined.
4. Press the mixture evenly into the bottom of the prepared pan. Bake for 10 minutes, then remove from the oven and let it cool completely while preparing the cake batter.

For the Cake:
1. In a small saucepan over low heat, melt the chocolate and butter together, stirring frequently until smooth. Remove from the heat and stir in the cocoa powder until fully incorporated.
2. In a large bowl, whisk together the sugar, eggs, vanilla, and salt until smooth. Stir in the melted chocolate mixture, then add the flour, whisking until everything is just combined.
3. Let the batter rest for 15 minutes to allow the flavors to meld together.
4. Pour the batter over the cooled crust and use an offset spatula to smooth the top. Bake for 22 to 27 minutes, until the edges are set and the center jiggles slightly. A toothpick inserted in the center should come out with moist crumbs.
5. Let the cake cool completely on a wire rack. Once cool, cover the pan with plastic wrap and refrigerate for at least 4 hours, or overnight.

For the Chocolate Mousse:
1. Heat 1 cup [240 g] of the heavy cream in a small saucepan over medium heat until just warmed.
2. In another saucepan, whisk the egg yolks together with the sugar and salt. Slowly pour the warmed cream over the egg mixture, whisking constantly to temper the eggs.
3. Cook the mixture over medium heat, stirring continuously until it thickens and coats the back of a spoon, about 3 to 5 minutes. Remove from the heat and strain through a fine-mesh sieve into a large bowl.
4. Stir in the vanilla and melted chocolate, whisking until smooth. Let cool to room temperature.

5. In the bowl of a stand mixer fitted with a whisk, whip the remaining ¾ cup [179 g] heavy cream until stiff peaks form. Gently fold one-third of the whipped cream into the chocolate custard, lightening the mixture, then fold in the remaining whipped cream.
6. Spread the chocolate mousse evenly over the chilled cake and use an offset spatula to smooth the top. Refrigerate for at least 8 hours, or overnight.

For the Ganache:
1. Place the chopped chocolate in a small bowl.
2. Heat the heavy cream in a small saucepan over medium-low heat until it begins to simmer.
3. Pour the hot cream over the chocolate and cover the bowl with plastic wrap. Let it sit for 5 minutes, then remove the wrap and stir the ganache until smooth. Allow the ganache to cool to room temperature.

To Assemble:
1. Pour the ganache over the top of the cake, spreading it with an offset spatula to the edges, making sure to create an even layer. Let the ganache set for a few minutes before dusting with cocoa powder.
2. Once the ganache is set, gently remove the cake from the springform pan. Slice and serve immediately, or refrigerate for up to 24 hours.

Variation:

Triple Chocolate Mint Mousse Cake:
- Add 1 teaspoon of mint extract to the cake base along with the vanilla.
- Before serving, top the cake with crushed candy cane pieces for a festive twist.

This cake is the ultimate indulgence for chocolate lovers. Whether you're sharing it with friends at a celebration or simply treating yourself to a moment of pure bliss, this mousse cake promises to deliver layers of flavor and rich chocolatey goodness in every bite.

Hazelnut Cheesecake with Chocolate Ganache

Ingredients

For the Crust:
- Chocolate wafer cookies: 2 cups (199 g)
- Cacao nibs: 1/4 cup (29 g)
- Unsalted butter: 4 tablespoons (57 g), melted, plus more for greasing the pan

For the Cheesecake:
- Cream cheese: 2 lb (908 g), at room temperature
- Granulated sugar: 1 1/2 cups (300 g)
- Salt: 1/2 teaspoon
- Sour cream: 1 cup (240 g), at room temperature
- Frangelico: 1/2 cup (119 g)
- Unsalted butter: 2 tablespoons, melted and cooled to room temperature

- Natural vanilla extract: 1 tablespoon
- Eggs: 3 large, plus 1 egg yolk, at room temperature
- Heavy cream: 3/4 cup (179 g), at room temperature

For the Ganache:
- Semisweet or bittersweet chocolate: 6 oz (169 g), finely chopped
- Heavy cream: 3/4 cup (179 g)

For Assembly:
- Sugared & Spiced Candied Nuts (hazelnut variation, chapter 5): for topping

Makes 8 to 12 servings

Directions

For the Crust
1. Preheat the oven to 325°F (165°C) and set the rack in the middle position. Grease a 9-inch (23 cm) springform pan.
2. In a food processor, pulse the chocolate wafer cookies and cacao nibs until they form fine crumbs.
3. Pour the melted butter over the crumbs and stir until well combined.
4. Press the mixture evenly into the bottom of the prepared pan. Bake for 10 minutes, then remove from the oven and let cool. Wrap the outer sides of the pan in two layers of aluminum foil, shiny side facing out, to keep the sides of the cheesecake from browning

For the Cheesecake
1. In the bowl of a stand mixer fitted with a paddle attachment, beat the cream cheese on medium speed for 4 to 5 minutes until light and completely smooth, scraping down the sides as needed.
2. Add the sugar and salt, and continue beating until fully incorporated and silky smooth, about 2 to 3 minutes.
3. Mix in the sour cream, Frangelico, melted butter, and vanilla, beating for another 2 to 3 minutes.
4. Add the eggs one at a time, followed by the yolk, beating just until each one is incorporated.
5. Slowly add the heavy cream, mixing on low speed until combined. Use a spatula to give the filling a final stir to ensure everything is evenly mixed.
6. Pour the filling over the cooled crust and smooth the top. Tap the pan gently on the counter to release any air bubbles.
7. Set a roasting pan filled with 4 quarts (3.8 L) of boiling water on the oven's lower rack.
8. Place the cheesecake on the rack above the water and bake for 1 hour without opening the oven door. The outer edges of the cheesecake should be firm, while the center remains slightly jiggly.
9. Turn off the oven, crack the door, and let the cheesecake rest in the warm oven for 30 minutes.
10. Transfer the pan to a wire rack and let cool for 5 to 10 minutes. Carefully remove the foil and run a thin knife around the edges to loosen the cheesecake. Let cool completely, then cover with parchment paper to prevent condensation and refrigerate for at least 6 hours or overnight.

For the Ganache

1. Place the chocolate in a small bowl.
2. In a small saucepan, heat the heavy cream over medium-low heat until it is simmering. Pour the hot cream over the chocolate and cover the bowl with plastic wrap. Let sit for 5 minutes.
3. Stir the ganache until smooth and shiny. Let it cool to room temperature before using. Stir occasionally to maintain a smooth texture.

Assembly

1. Remove the cheesecake from the pan by running a thin spatula between the sides of the cake and the pan, then gently remove the sides.
2. Slide the spatula under the crust and carefully transfer the cheesecake to a serving plate.
3. Pour the ganache over the top, using an offset spatula to spread it evenly. Add the candied nuts if desired.
4. Let the ganache set before serving. The cheesecake can be stored in the refrigerator for up to 1 day.

Notes:

- I've always found that using a water bath in the oven gives the cheesecake a smoother texture, but it's not necessary. The steam from a pan of water placed on the oven floor will prevent cracking without the hassle of submerging the cheesecake in a water bath.
- Baking times can vary. If your cheesecake hasn't set in the middle, don't worry—just bake it a bit longer. Using a thermometer to check the oven temperature and boiling water for the pan will also help achieve the best results. Don't be afraid to bake the cheesecake a bit longer if it hasn't fully set, as this won't affect the final texture.

Rustic Apple Pie with Caramel & Hard

Ingredients

For Filling:
- Gala apples: 2 1/2 lb [1.1 kg], peeled, cored, and sliced into 1/4 inch [6 mm] pieces (7 to 8 apples)
- Light brown sugar: 1/4 cup [49 g]
- Fresh lemon juice: 1 teaspoon
- Salt: 1/4 teaspoon
- Cornstarch: 2 tablespoons
- Ground cinnamon: 1/2 teaspoon
- Hard cider or apple cider: 1/2 cup [119 g]
- Homemade Caramel Sauce (chapter 5): 3/4 cup [162 g], at room temperature

For Crust:
- Homemade Pie Dough (chapter 2): 1 recipe
- All-purpose flour: for dusting

For Assembly:
- Egg wash
- Granulated sugar: 1 to 2 tablespoons
- Ice Cream Without the Churn (chapter 5) or Fluffy Homemade Whipped Cream (chapter 5): for serving

Makes 6 to 8 servings

Directions

1. **Prepare the filling:** In a large bowl, mix the apples, brown sugar, lemon juice, and salt. Let the mixture sit at room temperature for 1 to 2 hours, or cover and refrigerate it overnight. This will help the apples release their natural juices. Strain the liquid from the apples (you should have about 1/2 cup [119 g] of juice) and pour it into a medium saucepan. Return the apples to the bowl, then toss them with the cornstarch and cinnamon.
2. **Cook the apple juices:** Add the hard cider to the saucepan with the strained juice and bring it to a boil over medium heat. Reduce the heat to low and simmer until the liquid has reduced to about 1/2 cup [119 g], which will take 5 to 6 minutes. Remove from the heat and whisk in the caramel until smooth. Pour the caramel mixture over the apples and gently toss to coat. Set the filling aside while you roll out the pie dough.
3. **Prepare the dough:** Lightly flour your work surface and roll out one of the dough discs into a 12-inch [30.5 cm] circle, about 1/4 inch [6 mm] thick. Carefully transfer the dough into a 9-inch [23 cm] pie plate, gently pressing it into the bottom and sides. Place the pie plate in the fridge to chill while you roll out the second disc of dough.
4. **Assemble the pie:** Pour the prepared apple filling into the chilled pie shell, spreading it out evenly. Roll out the second piece of dough into another 12-inch [30.5 cm] circle and place it over the filling. Trim the excess dough to about 1 inch [2.5 cm] beyond the edge of the pie plate. Pinch the edges of the dough together and tuck it under itself to form a neat border, then crimp the edges. Cut four small slits in the center of the pie to allow steam to escape. Place the pie in the freezer to chill for 20 minutes while the oven preheats.
5. **Bake:** Preheat the oven to 425°F [220°C]. Place a sheet pan on the lowest oven rack to preheat (this helps crisp the bottom crust and catch any drips). Brush the top of the pie with egg wash and sprinkle generously with sugar. Transfer the pie to the preheated sheet pan and bake for 25 minutes. Reduce the oven temperature to 375°F [190°C] and continue baking for another 40 to 50 minutes, until the crust is golden and the filling is bubbling.
6. **Cool and serve:** Remove the pie from the oven and let it cool on a wire rack for at least 4 hours to allow the filling to set. Serve with a scoop of homemade ice cream or a dollop of whipped cream for a perfect finish. This pie is best enjoyed the same day it's made, when the flavors are freshest and the crust is still wonderfully crisp.

This pie is like a warm blanket on a cold day—a true comfort food that brings people together. The balance of sweet apples, rich caramel, and the slight tang from the cider makes it a pie that's not only delicious but also a little bit magical. Sharing it with loved ones is the ultimate way to celebrate the season.

Crème Brûlée Pumpkin Pie

Ingredients

For Pumpkin Filling:

- Unsalted butter: 3 tablespoons (45 g)
- Unsweetened pumpkin purée: one 15 oz (425 g) can
- Light brown sugar: 2 tablespoons
- Salt: 3/4 teaspoon
- Ground cinnamon: 1 teaspoon
- Ground ginger: 3/4 teaspoon
- Ground nutmeg: 1/2 teaspoon
- Ground cloves: a pinch
- Blackstrap rum (optional): 1 tablespoon
- Vanilla extract: 1 teaspoon
- Sweetened condensed milk: one 14 oz (396 g) can
- Eggs: 2 large, plus 2 large egg yolks, at room temperature
- Heavy cream: 1/2 cup (119 g)
- Lemon juice (optional): 1/2 teaspoon

For Assembly:

- Single Homemade Pie Dough (chapter 1): 1, fully baked and still warm
- Granulated sugar: 2 to 3 tablespoons
- Fluffy Homemade Whipped Cream (chapter 5): optional, for serving

Makes 6 to 8 servings

Directions

For the Pumpkin Filling

1. Preheat your oven to 400°F (200°C) and adjust a rack to the middle position. In a large, heavy-bottom saucepan over medium heat, brown the butter until it turns golden and fragrant. Then, stir in the pumpkin purée, brown sugar, salt, cinnamon, ginger, nutmeg, and cloves.
2. Let the mixture simmer for about 5 to 7 minutes, stirring occasionally, until it thickens and becomes shiny.
3. Remove the pan from the heat, and add the rum (if using) and vanilla extract. Mix well.
4. Return the pan to medium heat, and pour in the sweetened condensed milk, stirring until the mixture is smooth and combined. Whisk in the eggs, egg yolks, and heavy cream, and continue to mix until fully incorporated.
5. For an extra-smooth texture, strain the mixture through a fine-mesh sieve into a medium bowl, using a spatula to press the solids through the sieve.
6. If you find the flavor isn't bright enough, add ¼ teaspoon of lemon juice at a time, tasting as you go until you reach your desired balance.

To Assemble

7. Pour the filling into the warm, partially baked pie shell. Place the pie on a baking sheet and bake it for 10 minutes. Reduce the oven temperature to 300°F (150°C) and continue baking until the edges of the pie are puffed and the center jiggles only slightly when gently shaken, about 40 to 50 minutes.
8. Transfer the pie to a wire rack and let it cool to room temperature, which will take about 4 to 6 hours (though you can refrigerate it for several hours if serving later).
9. Just before serving, sprinkle a generous amount of granulated sugar over the entire surface of the pie.
10. Using a kitchen torch, brûlée the top until the sugar melts and forms a dark brown crust. If you prefer, you can slice the pie first, and brûlée each piece individually to make slicing less messy.

Serve immediately with whipped cream, if desired.

Creamy Chocolate Mint Ice Cream Pie

Ingredients

For Crust:
- Chocolate wafer cookies: 2 cups (199 g)
- Unsalted butter: 4 tablespoons (57 g), melted

For Meringue:
- Granulated sugar: 1 cup (199 g)
- Large egg whites: 3/4 cup (175 g), from 4 or 5 eggs, at room temperature
- Salt: 1/4 teaspoon
- Cream of tartar: 1/4 teaspoon
- Natural vanilla extract: 2 teaspoons

For Mint No-Churn Ice Cream:
- Sweetened condensed milk: one 14 oz (397 g) can
- Natural vanilla extract: 1 tablespoon
- Mint extract: 1 teaspoon (or more to taste)
- Salt: 1/4 teaspoon
- Cream cheese: 2 oz (57 g), at room temperature
- Heavy cream: 2 cups (240 g)
- Green food coloring: optional

Makes 6 to 8 servings

Directions

For the Crust
Preheat the oven to 350°F (180°C). Place the cookies in a food processor and pulse until they form fine crumbs. Transfer the crumbs to a medium bowl, pour in the melted butter, and stir with a spatula until everything is well combined. Press the mixture into the bottom and up the sides of a deep 9 ½ or 10-inch (24 or 25 cm) pie plate. Bake for 8 minutes, then remove from the oven and let cool completely.

For the Ice Cream
In a large bowl, whisk together the sweetened condensed milk, vanilla, mint extract, and salt until smooth. In the bowl of a stand mixer, beat the cream cheese on medium speed until smooth. Lower the speed, then slowly add the heavy cream in a steady stream, mixing until well combined. Increase the speed to medium-high and beat until stiff peaks form, about 3 to 4 minutes. Gently fold half of the whipped cream into the sweetened condensed milk mixture by hand, being careful not to deflate the cream. Add the remaining whipped cream, folding gently until smooth. If you're using food coloring, stir it in now. Pour the mixture into the prepared crust and freeze until firm, at least 6 hours, or up to 4 days.

For the Meringue
Pour 1 inch (2.5 cm) of water into a medium saucepan and bring it to a gentle simmer over medium heat. In the bowl of a stand mixer, combine the sugar, egg whites, salt, and cream of tartar. Set the bowl over the simmering water, making sure the water doesn't touch the bottom of the bowl. Stir constantly with a rubber spatula until the sugar dissolves and the mixture reaches 160°F (70°C), about 4 to 5 minutes. Remove the bowl from the heat and place it in the stand mixer. Whisk on low speed for 1 minute, then increase to medium-high and beat until stiff, glossy peaks form, about 8 to 10 minutes. The bowl should feel cool to the touch at this point. Add the vanilla and mix on medium-low speed until incorporated.

To Assemble
Remove the ice cream pie from the freezer. Quickly spread the meringue over the top using a spatula, creating decorative swirls with the back of a spoon. If you like, you can toast the meringue with a kitchen torch. Serve immediately or store the pie in the freezer with the meringue for up to 8 hours.

Variation:

Candy Cane Cake: Add ½ cup (100 g) crushed candy canes to the sweetened condensed milk mixture. Use pink food coloring instead of green, and sprinkle more crushed candy canes over the meringue.

Dark Chocolate Tart with a Hint of Irish Cream

Ingredients

For Chocolate Filling:
- Bittersweet or semisweet chocolate: 9 oz [255 g]
- Heavy cream: 3/4 cup [179 g]
- Irish cream (optional): 1/3 cup [79 g]
- Egg: 1 large, plus 2 large egg yolks, at room temperature
- Natural vanilla extract: 1 teaspoon
- Salt: 1/4 teaspoon

For Assembly:
- Shortbread Tart Crust: (chapter 2), baked and cooled
- Fluffy Homemade Whipped Cream (chapter 5), for serving

Makes One 10-inch Tart

Directions

Instructions:

1. **Preheat the Oven:** Adjust an oven rack to the middle position and preheat the oven to 350°F [180°C].
2. **Prepare the Filling:** Place the chocolate in a medium heatproof bowl. In a small saucepan over medium heat, bring the heavy cream to a gentle simmer, just until it's about to boil. Pour the hot cream over the chocolate and cover the bowl with plastic wrap. Let it sit for 5 minutes to allow the chocolate to melt. After 5 minutes, remove the plastic and whisk the mixture until smooth and fully combined. If you're using Irish cream, whisk it in at this point, followed by the eggs, egg yolks, vanilla extract, and salt.
3. **Assemble the Tart:** Pour the chocolate filling into the pre-baked and cooled shortbread crust, smoothing the top with a spatula if needed. Place the tart in the oven and bake for 15 to 18 minutes, or until the center of the filling is set but still has a slight jiggle when gently shaken—think Jell-O consistency.
4. **Cool and Serve:** Once baked, transfer the tart to a wire rack to cool to room temperature.
5. Serve slices with a generous dollop of whipped cream on the side. For the best texture and flavor, enjoy the tart the day it's baked. However, you can store any leftovers loosely covered in the refrigerator for up to 2 days.

This tart is perfect for when you want to impress your guests with minimal effort. The smooth, rich chocolate filling combined with the buttery, tender shortbread crust is sure to make everyone's taste buds sing with joy. If you like to add a touch of indulgence, the Irish cream will give it a subtle warmth that perfectly complements the deep chocolate flavor.

Chilled Chocolate Bonbons

Ingredients

- Ice Cream Without the Churn (any flavor, not yet frozen): 1 recipe (chapter 5)
- Semisweet or bittersweet chocolate: 12 oz [340 g], finely chopped

Makes 40 Bonbons

Directions

1. **Prepare the Bonbons:** Fill silicone molds (about 1 tablespoon in size for bite-size bonbons) with the unfrozen ice cream mixture. If you prefer larger molds, just be sure to melt additional chocolate later. Freeze the filled molds for at least 6 hours or overnight, until the ice cream is firm. No molds? No problem! Use a cookie scoop to make tablespoon-sized ice cream balls and place them on a lined baking sheet. Freeze until completely firm.
2. **Melt the Chocolate:** Once the ice cream is fully frozen, prepare a sheet pan lined with parchment paper. Let the ice cream re-firm in the freezer while you melt the chocolate. In a small saucepan over low heat, melt the chopped chocolate, stirring frequently until smooth. Pour the melted chocolate into a medium-sized bowl and allow it to cool for about 10 minutes.
3. **Coat the Bonbons:** Working quickly, remove one ice cream ball from the freezer and dip it into the melted chocolate. Use a skewer or fork to coat the bonbon evenly. Lift it out, let the excess chocolate drip back into the bowl, and place the coated bonbon on the lined sheet pan. Repeat with the remaining ice cream balls, transferring the pan to the freezer after each bonbon is coated to keep the ice cream firm.
4. **Freeze and Store:** Freeze the bonbons for an additional 20 to 30 minutes until the chocolate has hardened. They can be stored in the freezer for up to one week, ready to be enjoyed at any time!

Enjoy these delightful, chocolate-covered frozen treats, and don't hesitate to get creative with the toppings—whether it's crushed candy, sprinkles, or a dash of sea salt for a gourmet touch. It's a simple yet decadent way to bring a little joy to your holiday celebrations!

Shortbread Tart Crust

Ingredients

- Unsalted butter: 10 tablespoons (142 g), at room temperature
- Granulated sugar: 1/3 cup (65 g)
- Salt: 1/2 teaspoon
- Egg: 1 large, plus 1 large egg yolk
- Natural vanilla extract: 1 teaspoon
- All-purpose flour: 2 cups (284 g)
- Egg wash

Makes one 10-inch (25 cm) tart crust

Directions

1. **Making the dough:** In a large mixing bowl, beat the butter on low speed with an electric mixer until creamy, about 1 minute. Add the sugar and salt, continuing to beat on low speed for about 2 minutes until well combined. Be sure to scrape down the sides of the bowl to ensure everything is mixed in evenly.

2. **Adding the wet ingredients:** On low speed, add the egg, egg yolk, and vanilla extract, mixing until everything comes together smoothly. Now, add the flour and mix on low speed until the dough begins to come together.

3. **Shaping the dough:** Transfer the dough into a 10-inch (25 cm) tart pan with a removable bottom. Gently press the dough evenly into the bottom and up the sides of the pan with your hands. To make things easier, place the tart pan on a baking sheet and freeze the dough for 20-30 minutes until it's firm.

4. **Baking the crust:** Preheat your oven to 350°F (180°C). Remove the tart pan from the freezer and line it with parchment paper, making sure to cover the edges to prevent them from burning. Fill the center with pie weights and bake for 24-28 minutes, until the dough turns a light golden brown and is no longer wet to the touch.

5. **Finishing the crust:** Take the tart out of the oven, carefully remove the pie weights and parchment paper, and brush the center of the crust with egg wash. Place it back in the oven for another 3-6 minutes, until the center is a deep golden brown. Transfer the tart crust to a wire rack to cool completely before filling.

> **Note:**
> Tart pans come in many different depths, and some are quite shallow. For this recipe, you'll need a tart pan that is 1½ to 2 inches (4 to 5 cm) in height.

Homemade Pie Dough

Makes a Single 9-inch (23 cm) Pie

Ingredients

For the Crust:
- Unsalted butter: 8 tablespoons [1 stick or 114 g], cut into pieces
- All-purpose flour: 1 1/2 cups [213 g], plus more for dusting
- Granulated sugar: 1 tablespoon
- Salt: 1/2 teaspoon
- Ice water: 1 cup [240 g]

For a Double 9-inch [23 cm] Pie Crust:
- Unsalted butter: 18 tablespoons [2 1/4 sticks or 255 g], cut into pieces
- All-purpose flour: 2 1/2 cups [355 g], plus more for dusting
- Granulated sugar: 2 tablespoons
- Salt: 1 teaspoon
- Ice water: 1 cup [240 g]

Directions

1. Place the butter pieces in a small bowl and transfer it to the freezer for about 5-10 minutes to chill.
2. In the bowl of a stand mixer fitted with a paddle attachment, mix the flour, sugar, and salt on low speed until combined.
3. Add half of the chilled butter and mix on low speed until the butter starts to break down, about 1 minute.
4. Add the remaining butter and continue mixing until most of the butter is in pea-sized pieces.
5. While mixing on low speed, slowly drizzle in 1/4 cup [59 g] of ice water, just until the dough starts to come together but is still slightly crumbly. If it's too dry, add more water, 1 tablespoon at a time.
6. Turn the dough out onto a lightly floured surface and gently flatten it into a square shape.
7. Fold the dough over itself and flatten again. Repeat this process three or four times, gathering any loose pieces as you go.
8. Finally, form the dough into a 6-inch [15 cm] disk (if making a single crust) or two disks (for a double crust), wrap in plastic wrap, and refrigerate for at least 30 minutes, or up to 2 days before using.

For a Single Pie Crust:
1. Lightly flour a work surface and roll the dough into a 12-inch [30.5 cm] circle. Gently fold the dough into quarters and transfer it to a 9-inch [23 cm] pie plate. Unfold it, letting the excess drape over the edges.
2. Press the dough into the bottom and sides of the plate, trimming the excess to leave about 1 inch [2.5 cm] past the edge.
3. Chill the dough in the freezer for 20-30 minutes. Meanwhile, preheat your oven to 400°F [200°C] and place a sheet pan in the oven to preheat.

Partially Baked Crust:
Bake for 25-28 minutes, until lightly golden. Remove the pie weights and parchment paper, then continue with the rest of your pie recipe.

Fully Baked Crust:
Continue baking for an additional 8-12 minutes until golden brown. Transfer to a wire rack to cool completely.

To finish off, take a moment to admire your beautifully baked pie crust—flaky, golden, and ready to cradle whatever delicious filling you've prepared. With each step, you've put care and love into this classic recipe, and soon, your kitchen will be filled with the comforting warmth of a pie that's just as delightful to make as it is to share. Enjoy every bite!

3
Gifts of Delight

Homemade Caramel Candies

Ingredients

- Granulated sugar: 1 3/4 cups [349 g]
- Light corn syrup: 1/2 cup [159 g]
- Water: 1/4 cup [59 g]
- Salt: 1/2 teaspoon
- Heavy cream: 1 1/4 cups [300 g]
- Unsalted butter: 6 tablespoons [85 g], plus more for greasing the pan
- Natural vanilla extract: 1 tablespoon

Makes 24 Large or 48 Small Caramels

Directions

1. Grease an 8 x 4 in [20 x 10 cm] loaf pan and line it with a parchment sling, leaving an overhang on each side for easy removal. Grease the parchment paper as well.
2. In a large, heavy-bottom saucepan (make sure it's deep, as caramel tends to bubble up), combine the sugar, corn syrup, water, and salt. Stir gently, trying to avoid getting any sugar crystals on the sides of the pan.
3. Bring to a boil over medium-high heat, cover, and let cook until the sugar dissolves, about 3-5 minutes. Uncover and cook until the sugar turns a light golden color and reaches 300°F [150°C] on an instant-read thermometer, about 6-7 minutes.
4. Lower the heat to medium and cook until the sugar reaches a deeper golden hue and hits 340°F [170°C], about 4-5 minutes. Remove the pan from the heat and carefully add the cream and butter (it will bubble up, so be cautious). Return the pan to medium-high heat and cook until the caramel reaches your desired consistency: for soft, melt-in-your-mouth caramels, cook to 248°F [120°C], or for firmer, chewy caramels, cook to 252°F [122°C], stirring frequently, 4-7 minutes.
5. Stir in the vanilla and let the caramel sit for 2-3 minutes until the bubbles subside. Pour the caramel into the prepared pan, tapping it gently to release any air bubbles.
6. Let the caramel cool completely, then refrigerate for 1 hour. Using the parchment overhang, lift the caramel out of the pan. Cut in half lengthwise, then cut each half into 12 pieces for 24 rectangular candies. If you want smaller pieces, cut them in half again for a total of 48 candies. Wrap each caramel in wax paper or cellophane, twisting the ends to seal.
7. Store wrapped caramels in an airtight container at room temperature for up to two weeks.

Variations:

- **Orange Caramel**: Add 1 tablespoon of Triple Sec and 2 teaspoons of orange zest with the vanilla for a citrusy twist.

- **Espresso Caramel**: Stir in 1 teaspoon of finely ground espresso and 1 tablespoon of freshly brewed coffee along with the vanilla for a bold coffee flavor.

- **Salted Caramel**: Sprinkle each cut piece of caramel with a pinch of fleur de sel before wrapping for an irresistible salted caramel treat.

Peanut Butter Cups

Ingredients

- Semisweet or bittersweet chocolate: 16 oz (455 g)
- Creamy peanut butter: 1/2 cup (108 g)
- Confectioners' sugar: 1/4 cup (29 g)
- Unsalted butter: 2 tablespoons, at room temperature
- Natural vanilla extract: 1/2 teaspoon
- Salt: a pinch

Makes 16 Peanut Butter Cups

Directions

1. In a small saucepan over low heat, melt the chocolate, stirring frequently until smooth. Pour the melted chocolate into a medium bowl and let it cool for about 10 minutes.
2. Meanwhile, in another medium bowl, mix together the peanut butter, confectioners' sugar, butter, vanilla, and a pinch of salt until fully combined and smooth.
3. Pour about a tablespoon of chocolate into each cavity of a silicone mold (or line a mini muffin pan with paper liners). Tilt the mold to coat the sides with chocolate. Scoop out a scant tablespoon of the peanut butter mixture and gently roll it into a ball between your palms. If the mixture is too sticky, refrigerate it for about 10 minutes to firm up.
4. Place each peanut butter ball into the center of the chocolate molds, then top each one with more melted chocolate to cover. Gently tap the mold on the counter to smooth the tops, then place the mold in the refrigerator to chill for 2 to 3 hours until set.
5. Once the peanut butter cups are firm, pop them out of the molds and allow them to come to room temperature before serving. Store them in an airtight container in the refrigerator for up to one week.

Variations:

Cacao Nibs Topping: If you want to add a special touch, melt 1 oz (28 g) of chocolate and spoon ½ teaspoon over the top of each peanut butter cup. Smooth the surface and sprinkle with chopped cacao nibs. Let set before serving.

Triple Chocolate Peppermint Bark

Ingredients

- Bittersweet chocolate (60 to 70%): 8 oz (226 g), finely chopped
- Semisweet chocolate: 8 oz (226 g), finely chopped
- Heavy cream: 1/3 cup (79 g)
- Peppermint extract: 3/4 teaspoon
- White chocolate (good quality): 8 oz (226 g), finely chopped
- Candy canes or peppermint candies: 3, crushed (or a handful of peppermint candies, crushed)

Makes 30 to 40 Pieces

Directions

1. Using a pencil and ruler, mark a 9 by 13-inch (23 by 33 cm) rectangle on a piece of parchment paper. Flip the paper over so the pencil marks are on the bottom, and place it on a baking sheet.
2. Melt the bittersweet chocolate in a heatproof bowl over a saucepan of barely simmering water (making sure the bottom of the bowl doesn't touch the water). Stir occasionally until smooth and fully melted. Remove the bowl from the heat and pour the chocolate into the marked rectangle on the parchment. Use an offset spatula to spread the chocolate evenly. Chill in the fridge for about 15 minutes, until set.
3. In the same bowl, melt the semisweet chocolate with the cream and peppermint extract over barely simmering water, stirring frequently until smooth. Let the mixture cool to room temperature, about 15 minutes. Pour this over the chilled bittersweet chocolate layer and use the offset spatula to spread it evenly. Chill again for about 1 hour, until firm.
4. Melt the white chocolate in a clean bowl over simmering water until smooth. Working quickly, pour the white chocolate over the semisweet chocolate layer, using the spatula to spread it out. Sprinkle the crushed candy canes on top. Chill in the fridge for about 20 minutes, until firm.
5. Once firm, carefully transfer the parchment paper with the bark onto a cutting board. Trim any uneven edges, then cut the bark into 2 by 9-inch strips (5 by 23 cm). Slice the strips into smaller squares or triangles, whatever you prefer.

Store the bark at room temperature for 10 minutes before serving. To store long-term, place the bark in an airtight container with sheets of wax paper or parchment paper between layers so the pieces don't stick together. The bark can be kept in the fridge for up to 1 week.

Soft Red Velvet Cookies

Ingredients

- All-purpose flour: 1 1/2 cups (213 g)
- Baking powder: 1 teaspoon
- Baking soda: 1/8 teaspoon
- Granulated sugar: 3/4 cup plus 3 tablespoons (188 g)
- Light brown sugar: 1/2 cup (100 g), packed
- Eggs: 2 large, plus 2 large egg yolks, at room temperature
- Canola oil: 1 tablespoon
- Red velvet bakery emulsion or red food coloring: 1 tablespoon
- Natural vanilla extract: 1 teaspoon
- Salt: 1/2 teaspoon
- Unsalted butter: 4 tablespoons (57 g)
- Semisweet or bittersweet chocolate: 3 oz (85 g), finely chopped
- Cocoa powder: 1/4 cup (25 g)
- Confectioners' sugar: 1/2 cup (59 g), for rolling

Makes About 20 Cookies

Directions

1. Prep the Oven: Adjust an oven rack to the middle position and preheat your oven to 350°F (180°C). Line three baking sheets with parchment paper.
2. Mix Dry Ingredients: In a small bowl, whisk together the flour, baking powder, and baking soda.
3. Melt Chocolate and Butter: In a small saucepan, melt the butter and chocolate together over low heat, stirring frequently to prevent scorching. Once melted, remove from the heat and whisk in the cocoa powder until smooth. Set aside to cool slightly.
4. Prepare Wet Ingredients: In a large bowl, whisk together ¾ cup (149 g) granulated sugar, brown sugar, eggs, egg yolks, canola oil, red velvet emulsion, vanilla, and salt until well combined.
5. Combine Mixtures: Slowly pour the cooled chocolate mixture into the wet ingredients, whisking until fully incorporated. Add the dry ingredients, stirring gently with a rubber spatula until the dough comes together. Cover and refrigerate for at least 6 hours or overnight.
6. Shape the Dough: In a small bowl, combine the confectioners' sugar with the remaining 3 tablespoons of granulated sugar. Using a cookie scoop, portion the dough into 1 ½ tablespoon-sized balls. Roll each dough ball in the sugar mixture, making sure they're fully coated.
7. Bake: Place eight cookies on each prepared baking sheet, leaving space between them. Bake one sheet at a time, rotating halfway through baking. The cookies should be set on the edges but still soft in the center, about 12 to 14 minutes.
8. Cool and Store: Let the cookies cool on the sheet for a few minutes before transferring them to a wire rack to cool completely. Store the cookies in an airtight container at room temperature for up to 3 days.

Note:

The dough can be quite sticky, so using a cookie scoop is helpful. If the dough is too soft to handle, refrigerate it for an additional 15 minutes to make it easier to work with.

Caramel Pecan Delight Bars

Ingredients

For the Crust:
- Unsalted butter: 1 cup (2 sticks or 227 g), at room temperature
- Granulated sugar: 1 cup (199 g)
- Salt: 1/2 teaspoon
- Egg: 1 large
- Natural vanilla extract: 1 teaspoon
- All-purpose flour: 2 cups (284 g)
- Semisweet chocolate chips: 2 cups (359 g)

For the Caramel:
- Granulated sugar: 1 1/2 cups (300 g)
- Salt: 1/4 teaspoon
- Water: 1/4 cup (59 g)
- Corn syrup: 3 tablespoons
- Heavy cream: 1 1/4 cups (105 g)
- Unsalted butter: 2 tablespoons
- Natural vanilla extract: 1 teaspoon

For Assembly:
- Toasted pecan halves: 2 cups (279 g)

Makes 12 Large or 24 Small Bars

Directions

For the Crust:
1. Preheat the oven to 350°F (180°C). Line a 9 x 13 inch (23 x 33 cm) pan with parchment paper, leaving a little overhang on the sides for easy removal later.
2. In a large bowl, using a mixer, beat the butter on medium speed until creamy, about 1 minute. Add the sugar and salt, and continue beating until the mixture becomes light and fluffy, 2 to 3 minutes.
3. Beat in the egg and vanilla extract, then gradually add the flour and mix on low speed until the dough comes together.
4. Press the dough evenly into the prepared pan. Bake for 18-22 minutes, until the crust is golden and set.
5. Remove from the oven and immediately sprinkle the chocolate chips over the hot crust. Return to the oven for 2 minutes, just enough for the chocolate to melt slightly.
6. Use an offset spatula to spread the melted chocolate evenly over the crust, then set aside to cool completely.

For the Caramel:
1. In a large heavy-bottom saucepan, combine the sugar, salt, water, and corn syrup. Stir gently and cover the pan, bringing the mixture to a boil over medium-high heat.
2. Once the sugar has dissolved, uncover and cook until the mixture turns a light golden color and reaches 300°F (150°C), about 4 to 5 minutes.
3. Lower the heat slightly and cook until the caramel becomes a deep golden color and reaches 350°F (180°C), another 4 to 5 minutes.
4. Remove from heat and carefully pour in the heavy cream (it will foam up, so be cautious). Stir to combine, then add the butter and vanilla. Stir again until smooth and let the caramel cool for 5 to 10 minutes.

For Assemble the Bars:
1. Pour the warm caramel evenly over the cooled chocolate crust.
2. Gently press the toasted pecan halves into the caramel, ensuring they're evenly distributed.
3. Let the bars sit at room temperature until the caramel is set. Once firm, use the parchment overhang to lift the bars from the pan, and cut them into squares or bars.
4. Store the bars in an airtight container in the fridge for 2 to 3 days, or enjoy them right away!

These Caramel Bars are the perfect combination of rich caramel, smooth chocolate, and crunchy pecans—a delicious holiday treat that's sure to become a favorite in your home, too!

Chocolate Gift Cakes

Ingredients

For the Chocolate Cake:
- Sour cream: 1/2 cup [119 g], at room temperature
- Whole milk: 1/2 cup [119 g], at room temperature
- Canola oil: 1/2 cup [112 g]
- Eggs: 3 large, at room temperature
- Natural vanilla extract: 1 teaspoon
- All-purpose flour: 2 cups [284 g]
- Granulated sugar: 1 cup [199 g]
- Light brown sugar: 1 cup [199 g]
- Dutch-process cocoa powder: 3/4 cup [75 g]
- Baking soda: 2 teaspoons

- Baking powder: 1 teaspoon
- Salt: 1 teaspoon
- Hot, freshly brewed coffee: 1 cup [240 g]

For the Chocolate Buttercream:
- Semisweet or bittersweet chocolate: 8 oz [226 g]
- Unsalted butter: 1 1/2 cups [3 sticks or 339 g], at room temperature
- Salt: a pinch
- Corn syrup: 3 tablespoons
- Natural vanilla extract: 2 teaspoons
- Confectioners' sugar: 2 cups [240 g]

Makes 3 6-inch (15 cm) Cakes

Directions

for the Cake

1. Preheat the oven to 350°F [180°C]. Grease three 6 by 2-inch [15 by 5 cm] cake pans and line the bottoms with parchment paper.
2. In a medium bowl or liquid measuring cup, combine the sour cream, milk, oil, eggs, and vanilla.
3. In the bowl of a stand mixer, mix together the flour, granulated sugar, brown sugar, cocoa powder, baking soda, baking powder, and salt.
4. With the mixer on low speed, slowly add the milk mixture. Increase the speed to medium and mix until combined, about 20-30 seconds.
5. Slowly pour in the hot coffee, mixing until just combined. Make sure to give the batter a quick stir with a spatula to ensure everything is well incorporated.
6. Divide the batter evenly among the prepared pans. Bake for 25-35 minutes, or until a toothpick inserted into the center comes out with just a few crumbs attached.
7. Let the cakes cool in the pans for about 30 minutes before transferring them to a wire rack to cool completely. Once cool, the cakes can be frosted or wrapped in plastic wrap and refrigerated overnight.

For the Chocolate Buttercream

1. Pour about 1 inch [2.5 cm] of water into a medium saucepan and bring it to a gentle simmer. Melt the chocolate in a heatproof bowl set over the simmering water, making sure the bottom of the bowl doesn't touch the water. Stir constantly until smooth, then set aside to cool slightly.
2. In the bowl of a stand mixer, beat the butter and salt on medium speed until light and fluffy, about 3 minutes.
3. Add the corn syrup and vanilla extract and continue beating until combined.
4. Lower the speed and gradually add the confectioners' sugar, beating on medium speed until smooth and creamy, 2-3 minutes.
5. Add the melted chocolate and mix on low speed until no streaks remain, scraping down the sides of the bowl as needed.

To Assemble

1. Divide the chocolate buttercream evenly between the three cakes. Using an offset spatula, spread it smoothly over the tops of the cakes.
2. The cakes can be covered and stored in the refrigerator for up to 24 hours. Be sure to bring them to room temperature before serving to let the rich chocolate flavor really shine.

These cakes are not only delicious but also a sweet way to share joy during the colder months. Their rich chocolatey flavor will leave a lasting impression, and maybe, just maybe, you'll keep one as a little gift to yourself!

Mini Fruit Cakes

Ingredients

For the Candied Cherries:
- Granulated sugar: 1 1/2 cups [300 g]
- Kirsch: 3 tablespoons
- Salt: 1/4 teaspoon
- Frozen sour cherries: 2 cups [279 g], thawed overnight in a plastic bag with juices reserved.

For the Cake:
- Egg whites: 1/2 cup [105 g], from about 3 or 4 large eggs
- Whole milk: 1/2 cup [119 g], at room temperature
- Homemade French Crème Fraîche (chapter 5) or sour cream: 2 tablespoons, at room temperature
- Triple sec: 1 tablespoon
- Natural vanilla extract: 1 1/2 teaspoons
- Almond extract: 1 teaspoon
- All-purpose flour: 1 1/3 cups + 1 tablespoon [199 g]
- Granulated sugar: 1 cup [199 g]
- Orange zest: 1 tablespoon
- Baking powder: 2 teaspoons
- Salt: 1/2 teaspoon
- Unsalted butter: 8 tablespoons [114 g], at room temperature, cut into 8 pieces, plus more for greasing the pan
- Sugary Citrus Peel Delights (chapter 5) or store-bought candied peel: 1/2 cup [70 g]
- Dried fruit (such as papaya, apricots, cranberries, etc.; optional): 1/2 cup [70 g]

For the Chocolate Coating:
- Semisweet or bittersweet chocolate: 14 oz [397 g], finely chopped
- Shortening: 2 oz [57 g]
- Edible gold leaf: for garnish

Make 24 Mini Fruit Cakes

Directions

For the Cherries

In a large, heavy-bottomed saucepan over medium heat, combine the sugar, kirsch, salt, and cherry juice. Cook until the sugar is dissolved, about 3-4 minutes. Add the sour cherries, increase the heat to medium-high, and bring to a boil. Cover the pan, lower the heat to medium-low, and let the cherries simmer for 45 minutes, stirring occasionally, until they are wrinkled but still firm. The syrup should reach around 235°F [113°C]. Allow to cool to room temperature. Once cooled, remove the cherries from the liquid and transfer them to a parchment-lined sheet pan if using immediately, or store them in an airtight container in the refrigerator for up to 4 months. The cherry syrup can also be stored in an airtight container in the refrigerator for the same amount of time.

For the Cake

Preheat your oven to 350°F [180°C] and position the rack in the center. Grease a 9x13-inch [23x33 cm] baking pan and line it with parchment paper. In a medium bowl, whisk together the egg whites, milk, crème fraîche, triple sec, vanilla, and almond extract. In a large mixing bowl, sift together the flour, sugar, orange zest, baking powder, and salt. With a mixer on low speed, add the butter, one piece at a time, until the mixture resembles coarse sand. Gradually add the wet ingredients, mixing until smooth. Gently fold in the candied cherries, orange peel, and dried fruit, if using. Pour the batter into the prepared pan, smoothing the top. Bake for 18-24 minutes, or until a skewer inserted in the center comes out clean. Allow the cake to cool completely, then use a 2-inch [5 cm] cutter to make small rounds.

For Preparing the Chocolate Coating

In a small saucepan over low heat, melt 12 oz [340 g] of the chocolate with the shortening, stirring until smooth. Remove from the heat and add the remaining 2 oz [57 g] of chocolate, stirring until fully melted and glossy.

For Assembling the Cakes

Line a sheet pan with parchment paper and set a greased wire rack over it. Take one cake round at a time, place it on a fork, and dip it into the melted chocolate, coating the entire cake and letting any excess drip back into the saucepan. Transfer each coated cake to the wire rack and let them sit at room temperature until the chocolate is set. If you wish, add a light touch of edible gold leaf for decoration. Store the cakes in an airtight container at room temperature for up to 2 days.

Note: The cherries should release quite a bit of juice as they thaw. If they don't, add ½ cup [119 g] of water to the saucepan.

Crunchy Orange-Almond Treats

Ingredients

For the Buttery Shortbread Crust:
- Unsalted butter: 12 tablespoons [1 1/2 sticks or 169 g], at room temperature, plus extra for greasing the pan
- Granulated sugar: 1/2 cup [100 g]
- Salt: 1/2 teaspoon
- Grated orange zest: 2 teaspoons
- Egg yolks: 2 large, at room temperature
- Natural vanilla extract: 1 teaspoon
- All-purpose flour: 1 1/2 cups [213 g], plus extra for dusting

For the Orange-Almond Filling:
- Heavy cream: 1/2 cup [119 g]
- Granulated sugar: 1/3 cup [65 g]
- Light corn syrup: 1/4 cup [79 g]
- Salt: 1/4 teaspoon
- Unsalted butter: 4 tablespoons [57 g]
- Triple sec: 3 tablespoons
- Natural vanilla extract: 1 teaspoon
- Sliced almonds: 2 cups [199 g]
- Chopped candied orange peels: 1/4 cup [74 g]

For Assembly and Chocolate Coating:
- Semisweet or bittersweet chocolate: 10 oz [284 g]

Make 12 Large or
16 Small Florentines

Directions

For Preparing the Shortbread Crust
Preheat your oven to 350°F [180°C] and position the rack in the center. Grease and line the bottom of a quarter sheet pan (9 x 13 in [23 x 33 cm]) with parchment paper. In a large bowl, beat the butter at low speed for about a minute until creamy. Add the sugar, salt, and orange zest, and continue to mix on medium speed until the mixture is light and fluffy, about 2-3 minutes. Add the egg yolks and vanilla, mixing just until combined. Gradually add the flour on low speed, blending until a soft dough forms.

Transfer the dough to a lightly floured work surface and gently shape it into a rectangle. Press the dough evenly into the prepared pan, making sure it fills the bottom and reaches the edges without going up the sides. Cover the dough with plastic wrap, pressing it gently to smooth the surface. Freeze the dough for 15 minutes, or until it feels firm to the touch.

Remove the pan from the freezer. Cover the dough with parchment paper and place another quarter sheet pan or pie weights on top to keep it from puffing up during baking. Bake the crust for 10-15 minutes, or until it turns a light golden color. Remove it from the oven, take off the weights, and let the crust cool completely in the pan. Lower the oven temperature to 325°F [165°C].

For the Orange-Almond Filling
While the crust is cooling, prepare the filling. In a medium saucepan over medium heat, combine the heavy cream, sugar, corn syrup, and salt. Cook, stirring occasionally, until the sugar dissolves. Increase the heat to medium-high and continue cooking until the mixture reaches 248°F [120°C], about 5-6 minutes, bubbling up before it settles back down. Remove the saucepan from the heat and add the butter, triple sec, and vanilla, swirling to combine. Stir in the almonds and candied orange peel until well mixed.

For Assembling and Baking
Pour the filling over the cooled crust and spread evenly. Bake for 25-30 minutes, rotating halfway, until golden brown (edges may darken but can be trimmed). Remove from the oven, place on a wire rack, and loosen edges with a spatula. Repeat after 5 minutes, then cool completely.

Chocolate Coating and Finishing Touches
Melt 8 oz (226 g) of chocolate in a small saucepan over low heat, stirring until smooth. Remove from heat, add the remaining 2 oz (57 g), and stir until fully melted. Line a baking sheet with parchment paper and set a wire rack on top. Invert the cooled bars onto the rack, filling side down, and pour the melted chocolate over, spreading it evenly. Use a baking comb to create decorative lines if desired. Let the chocolate set at room temperature. Once hardened, trim the edges with a serrated knife if needed and cut into 12 or 16 squares.

Vanilla Bean Shortbread Treats

Ingredients

- Unsalted butter: 1 cup [2 sticks or 227 g], at room temperature
- Granulated sugar: 2/3 cup [129 g], plus more for sprinkling
- Confectioners' sugar: 1/3 cup [40 g]
- Salt: 1 teaspoon
- Vanilla bean (seeds scraped) or Natural vanilla extract: 1 teaspoon
- Egg yolks: 2 large
- All-purpose flour: 2 cups [284 g], plus more for dusting
- Turbinado or sanding sugar: 1 cup [199 g], for sprinkling

Makes about 30 Cookies

Directions

1. In the bowl of a stand mixer fitted with the paddle attachment, beat the butter on medium speed until smooth and creamy, about 1 minute. Add the granulated sugar, confectioners' sugar, salt, and vanilla bean seeds (or vanilla extract). Continue mixing on medium speed until everything is well combined and the mixture looks creamy, about 2-3 minutes.
2. Add the egg yolks and mix on low speed until just blended. Add the flour and mix again on low speed until the dough comes together.
3. Lightly flour your work surface and transfer the dough to it. Shape the dough into a 12-inch [30.5 cm] log. Place the log on a piece of plastic wrap slightly longer than the dough. Sprinkle the turbinado sugar along the outside of the log, gently pressing it into the dough with your hands.
4. Wrap the log tightly in plastic wrap and refrigerate until firm, about 2 hours or overnight.
5. When you're ready to bake, adjust an oven rack to the middle position and preheat the oven to 350°F [180°C]. Line three baking sheets with parchment paper. Unwrap the chilled dough and slice it into ½-inch [12 mm] rounds, spacing the slices about 2 inches [5 cm] apart on the baking sheets.
6. Bake one sheet at a time, rotating halfway through, for 14-16 minutes, or until the edges are a light golden color while the centers stay pale. Transfer the cookies to a wire rack to cool completely. Store them in an airtight container at room temperature for up to 3 days.

Flavor Twists - These cookies are incredibly versatile! Try these fun variations to add a special twist:

Zesty Citrus
Add 2 teaspoons of finely grated citrus zest (lemon, lime, orange, or grapefruit) to the dough with the salt. For a little extra texture, you can add 1 tablespoon of poppy seeds along with the flour.

Rosemary Chocolate Chip
Mix in ½ cup [90 g] mini chocolate chips (or finely chopped chocolate) and 2 teaspoons minced rosemary after adding the flour, stirring gently to blend.

Pistachio Perfection
For a nutty variation, add ⅓ cup [40 g] chopped pistachios after incorporating the flour, folding gently to combine.

Cacao Nib and Caramelized White Chocolate
Add ½ cup [59 g] chopped cacao nibs and 1 oz [29 g] finely chopped caramelized white chocolate after adding the flour, folding carefully to blend.

Holiday Cut-Out Cookies

Ingredients

- **For the Cookie:**
- All-purpose flour: 4 cups [568 g], plus more for dusting
- Salt: 1 teaspoon
- Baking powder: 3/4 teaspoon
- Baking soda: 1/4 teaspoon
- Unsalted butter: 1 1/2 cups [3 sticks or 339 g], at room temperature
- Refined coconut oil: 3 tablespoons, at room temperature
- Granulated sugar: 1 3/4 cups [349 g]
- Egg: 1 large, plus 1 large egg yolk, at room temperature
- Natural vanilla extract: 1 tablespoon

For the Simple Glaze:
- Confectioners' sugar: 2 cups [240 g]
- Unsalted butter: 1 tablespoon, melted
- Natural vanilla extract: 1 teaspoon
- Salt: a pinch
- Water: 3 to 6 tablespoons [45 to 79 g]
- Food coloring: optional

For the Freeze-Dried Sugar Coating:
- Granulated sugar: 1 cup [199 g]
- Freeze-dried berries (such as strawberries or raspberries): 1 to 2 cups [32 to 64 g], adjust based on desired flavor and color

Make about 5 Dozen Cookies

Directions

1. In a large bowl, whisk together the flour, salt, baking powder, and baking soda. In the bowl of a stand mixer fitted with the paddle attachment, beat the butter on medium speed until creamy, about 1 minute. Add the coconut oil and continue mixing on medium speed until smooth. Add the granulated sugar and mix until light and fluffy, about 3-5 minutes.
2. Add the egg, egg yolk, and vanilla, mixing on low speed until combined. Gradually add the flour mixture, continuing to mix on low speed until everything is fully incorporated. Use a spatula to fold in any dry bits of dough that may remain at the bottom of the bowl.
3. Divide the dough in half. You can use it immediately or wrap each half in plastic wrap and refrigerate for up to 4 days (just let it come to room temperature before rolling).
4. When ready to bake, adjust your oven rack to the middle position and preheat to 350°F [180°C]. Line several baking sheets with parchment paper. On a lightly floured surface, roll out the dough to a thickness between ⅛ inch [4 mm] and ¼ inch [6 mm], depending on your preference for a softer or crisper cookie.
5. Using your favorite cookie cutters, cut out shapes, then carefully slide a spatula underneath each one and transfer to the prepared baking sheets, leaving 1 inch [2.5 cm] of space between each cookie. Chill the sheets of cookies in the refrigerator for 15 minutes before baking. You can re-roll any scraps of dough and cut out additional shapes.
6. Bake one sheet at a time, 12-16 minutes, or until the cookies are cooked through. For softer cookies, bake for about 12 minutes; for crisper cookies, bake a bit longer until the edges are a light golden brown. Let the cookies cool completely on the baking sheets before decorating.

Making the Simple Glaze

In a medium bowl, combine the confectioners' sugar, melted butter, vanilla, salt, and 3 tablespoons of water, stirring until smooth. If the glaze is too thick, add additional water, one tablespoon at a time, until you reach your desired consistency. For a pop of color, you can add food coloring to the glaze.

Spread the glaze over the cooled cookies, allowing it to set fully. Once set, the cookies can be stored in an airtight container at room temperature for up to 3 days.

Freeze-Dried Sugar Coating

In a food processor, combine the freeze-dried berries and granulated sugar, processing until the berries are finely ground and well mixed with the sugar, about 30 seconds. Sprinkle the berry-sugar mixture over the tops of the cookies, gently pressing it onto the surface, and shake off any excess. These sugar-coated cookies can also be stored in an airtight container at room temperature for up to 3 days.

4
Not Just Christmas

All-in-One Bundt Cake

Ingredients

- All-purpose flour: 3 cups [426 g]
- Baking soda: 1/2 teaspoon
- Sour cream: 1/2 cup [119 g], at room temperature
- Whole milk: 1/2 cup [119 g], at room temperature
- Unsalted butter: 1 1/4 cups [2 1/2 sticks or 284 g], at room temperature, plus extra for greasing the pan
- Granulated sugar: 3 cups [599 g]
- Salt: 1 1/4 teaspoons
- Eggs: 6 large, at room temperature
- Canola oil: 2 tablespoons
- Natural vanilla extract: 1 tablespoon

Make 8 to 12 Servings

Directions

1. Position a rack in the middle of your oven and preheat it to 350°F [180°C]. Grease a 10-inch [25 cm] Bundt pan generously with butter or non-stick spray, making sure every nook and cranny is coated.
2. In a medium bowl, whisk together the flour and baking soda, ensuring it's evenly mixed. In a separate bowl or a large measuring cup, stir together the sour cream and milk until smooth.
3. In the bowl of a stand mixer fitted with the paddle attachment, beat the butter on medium speed until creamy, about 1 minute. Add the sugar and salt, and continue beating on medium speed until the mixture is light and fluffy, about 4 to 6 minutes. This step is essential for achieving the cake's airy texture.
4. Scrape down the sides of the bowl. Add the eggs one at a time, beating on medium speed and scraping the bowl after each addition to ensure the batter remains smooth. Add the canola oil and vanilla, mixing on low speed until incorporated.
5. With the mixer on low speed, add half of the flour mixture and mix until just combined. Then, add the sour cream mixture and mix until smooth. Scrape down the sides, add the remaining flour mixture, and mix on low speed until everything is well blended. Finally, increase the speed to medium and beat for another 15 to 20 seconds to give the batter a final, light texture.
6. Pour the batter into the prepared Bundt pan, using a spatula to spread it evenly. Bake for 50 to 65 minutes, or until a wooden skewer inserted near the center comes out clean. Once done, transfer the pan to a wire rack and let it cool for 20 minutes. Carefully run a knife around the edges to loosen, then invert the cake onto the rack and lift off the pan. Let it cool completely before serving.
7. Wrapped in plastic, this cake can be stored at room temperature for 2 days or refrigerated for up to 4 days. It actually tastes better the day after baking, making it a wonderful make-ahead dessert.

Quick Tip: Greasing a Bundt Pan

If you've ever struggled with a Bundt cake sticking to the pan, a generous coat of grease and a parchment paper lining at the bottom can help, especially with intricate designs. I prefer using a 16-cup (3.8 L) pan with a flat bottom for recipes like this, as extra add-ins can increase sticking risk.

Variations:

Cream Cheese
Replace 1 ¼ cups [2 ½ sticks or 300 g] of butter with 1 cup [2 sticks or 227 g] unsalted butter and 6 oz [169 g] cream cheese, both at room temperature. Beat the cream cheese and butter together until smooth before adding the sugar.

Lemon Poppy Seed
Whisk 3 tablespoons of poppy seeds with the flour mixture. Add 2 tablespoons of grated lemon zest to the sugar, and replace ¼ cup [59 g] of the milk with ¼ cup [59 g] of fresh lemon juice for a refreshing twist.

Brown Sugar-Chocolate
Replace 2 cups [399 g] of the granulated sugar with brown sugar. Add 1 cup [179 g] of mini chocolate chips after adding the flour, stirring gently to combine.

Lemon Pull-Apart Bread

Ingredients

For the Bread:
- Eggs: 3 large, at room temperature
- Whole milk: 1/2 cup [119 g], warmed (100°F to 110°F [35°C to 45°C])
- Honey: 2 tablespoons
- Granulated sugar: 1 tablespoon
- All-purpose flour: 3 cups plus 2 tablespoons [443 g], plus extra for dusting
- Instant yeast: 2 teaspoons
- Salt: 1 1/2 teaspoons
- Unsalted butter: 8 tablespoons [1 stick or 114 g], at room temperature, cut into 8 pieces, plus more for greasing the pan

For the Filling:
- Granulated sugar: 3/4 cup [149 g]
- Lemon zest: 2 tablespoons
- Salt: a pinch
- Unsalted butter: 2 tablespoons, melted and slightly cooled

For the Icing:
- Confectioners' sugar: 1 1/2 cups [179 g]
- Fresh lemon juice: 2 to 4 tablespoons [30 to 59 g]
- Unsalted butter: 1 tablespoon, melted
- Natural vanilla extract: 1 teaspoon

Make one 9-Inch (23 cm) Loaf

Directions

For Making the Bread

1. Grease a large bowl and set aside. In a large liquid measuring cup, whisk together the eggs, warm milk, honey, and sugar until smooth.
2. In the bowl of a stand mixer fitted with the paddle attachment, mix the flour, yeast, and salt on low speed until combined. Add the egg mixture to the flour mixture and mix on low speed until a dough begins to form. If the dough feels dry, add 1 to 2 tablespoons of water to help it come together.
3. With the mixer on low, add the butter pieces one at a time, waiting until each piece is fully incorporated before adding the next. Once all the butter has been added, increase the speed to medium and continue mixing until the dough is smooth, about 1 minute. The dough will be sticky, so use a spatula to transfer it to the prepared bowl.
4. Cover the bowl with plastic wrap and let the dough rise for 30 minutes. Then, with dampened fingers or a spatula, gently pull the dough up from the bottom of the bowl and fold it over itself. Rotate the bowl slightly and repeat this folding motion six to eight more times, until all the dough has been folded over. Cover and let the dough rise for another 30 minutes. Repeat this folding process three more times, allowing the dough to rise for a total of 2 hours. For a deeper flavor, refrigerate the dough overnight or up to 72 hours.

Preparing the Filling

In a small bowl, mix together the granulated sugar, lemon zest, and a pinch of salt, pressing the zest into the sugar to release its oils. This will intensify the lemony flavor.

Assembling and Baking

1. Position an oven rack in the middle of your oven and preheat to 350°F [180°C]. Line a 9 by 4 by 4-inch [23 by 10 by 10 cm] Pullman pan with parchment paper.
2. On a lightly floured surface, roll the dough into a 20 by 12-inch [50 by 30.5 cm] rectangle, with a short side facing you. Brush the dough with the melted butter, then sprinkle the lemon-sugar mixture evenly over the dough, pressing it gently into the surface.
3. Using a pizza cutter or sharp knife, cut the dough crosswise into five strips (each about 12 by 4 inches [30.5 by 10 cm]). Stack the strips on top of each other, then cut the stack into six equal sections, each about 4 by 2 inches [10 by 5 cm]. Fit the layered sections into the prepared loaf pan, standing upright, with the cut edges facing up. Cover the pan loosely with plastic wrap and let the dough rise in a warm place until almost doubled, about 45 to 60 minutes.

4. Using a pizza cutter or sharp knife, cut the dough crosswise into five strips (each about 12 by 4 inches [30.5 by 10 cm]). Stack the strips on top of each other, then cut the stack into six equal sections, each about 4 by 2 inches [10 by 5 cm]. Fit the layered sections into the prepared loaf pan, standing upright, with the cut edges facing up. Cover the pan loosely with plastic wrap and let the dough rise in a warm place until almost doubled, about 45 to 60 minutes.

5. Place a baking sheet on a lower rack to catch any drips, then bake the bread for 40 to 50 minutes, or until the top is golden and an instant-read thermometer reads 195°F [91°C]. Check halfway through baking, and if the top is browning too quickly, cover with foil. Transfer the pan to a wire rack and allow the bread to cool for 20 minutes.

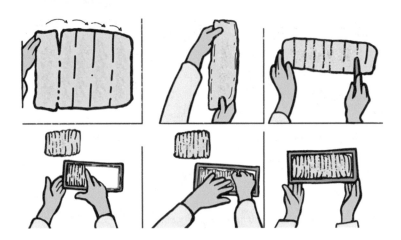

Making the Icing

While the bread is cooling, whisk together the confectioners' sugar, 2 tablespoons lemon juice, melted butter, and vanilla until smooth. Add more lemon juice, 1 tablespoon at a time, until the icing reaches your desired consistency.

Finishing Touches

After cooling slightly, pour half of the icing over the bread, allowing it to soak in for 15 minutes. Gently remove the loaf from the pan, drizzle the remaining icing over the top, and let cool slightly before serving. This bread is best enjoyed the day it's made, warm and fresh, with every layer pulling apart easily.

Make It Ahead

For a slow-rise option, prepare the dough as instructed but skip the final 45-minute rise. Instead, cover the loaf pan loosely with plastic wrap and refrigerate for up to 18 hours. When ready to bake, let the bread sit at room temperature for 45 minutes to 1 hour before baking.

Variations:

Cinnamon Pull-Apart Bread
Replace the lemon zest in the filling with 2 tablespoons of ground cinnamon. Omit the lemon juice in the icing and use water instead for a cozy, cinnamon flavor.
Orange Pull-Apart Bread
Substitute the lemon zest and juice with fresh orange zest and juice for a sweeter, milder citrus twist.

Crispy Blood Orange Turnovers

Ingredients

For the Cream Cheese Filling:
- Cream cheese: 4 oz [114 g], at room temperature
- Granulated sugar: 2 tablespoons
- Natural vanilla extract: 1/2 teaspoon
- Salt: a pinch
- Fresh lemon juice: 1 teaspoon

For Assembly:
- All-purpose flour: for dusting
- Quick and Easy Puff Pastry (chapter 4), cut into two pieces, or store-bought puff pastry: 1 lb [454 g]
- Blood Orange Curd (the variation of Silky Lemon Curd - chapter 5) or any jam of choice: 1/2 cup [159 g]
- Egg wash
- Granulated sugar: for sprinkling

Makes 8 Turnovers

Directions

For Making the Cream Cheese Filling

In the bowl of a stand mixer fitted with the paddle attachment, beat the cream cheese, sugar, vanilla, and salt on low speed until smooth, about 1 minute. Scrape down the sides of the bowl, then add ¼ teaspoon of the lemon juice and mix on low speed until combined. The lemon juice should enhance the flavor without overwhelming it. If you'd like a brighter flavor, add a little more juice, tasting as you go. Once done, transfer the filling to a small bowl, cover with plastic wrap, and refrigerate until ready to use.

For Assembling the Turnovers

Place a rack in the middle of the oven and preheat to 400°F [200°C]. Stack two baking sheets on top of each other and line the top sheet with parchment paper to prevent the bottoms of the turnovers from over-browning.

Lightly flour a clean work surface, then roll each piece of puff pastry into a 10-inch [25 cm] square. Cut each square into four 5-inch [12 cm] squares, giving you a total of eight squares.

Add a dollop of cream cheese filling and a tablespoon of blood orange curd to the center of each square. Fold each square into a triangle, gently pressing down the edges to seal. Use a fork to crimp the edges, ensuring a secure seal. Transfer the turnovers to the prepared baking sheet and freeze for 15 minutes to help the dough hold its shape during baking.

Brush the tops of the turnovers with egg wash, then generously sprinkle with granulated sugar for a sweet, golden finish. Bake for 20 to 25 minutes, rotating the pan halfway through, until the turnovers are puffed and golden brown. Remove from the oven and let them cool on a wire rack. These turnovers are best enjoyed warm, preferably the same day they're made.

These turnovers are a joy to make and share. Their golden, flaky layers and bright, creamy filling make every bite feel like a little celebration. Perfect for a cozy gathering or simply as a special treat to savor with a cup of tea, these turnovers bring warmth and cheer to any table. Enjoy!

Tropical Passion Fruit and Poppy Seed Muffins

Make 12 Large Muffins

Ingredients

For the Muffins:
- Large egg whites: 1 scant cup [211 g], from 6 or 7 eggs, at room temperature
- Sour cream: 3/4 cup [179 g], at room temperature
- Passion fruit purée: 3/4 cup [179 g], at room temperature
- Natural vanilla extract: 1 tablespoon
- All-purpose flour: 2 3/4 cups [391 g]
- Granulated sugar: 2 cups [399 g]
- Baking powder: 4 teaspoons
- Salt: 1 teaspoon
- Unsalted butter: 1 cup [2 sticks or 227 g], at room temperature, cut into 1-inch [2.5 cm] pieces
- Poppy seeds: 2 tablespoons, plus extra for sprinkling

For the Passion Fruit Icing:
- Confectioners' sugar: 1 1/2 cups [179 g]
- Passion fruit purée: 2 to 4 tablespoons [30 to 59 g]
- Unsalted butter: 1 tablespoon, melted
- Natural vanilla extract: 1/2 teaspoon

Directions

For Making the Muffins

Position a rack in the middle of your oven and preheat to 350°F [180°C]. Grease or line two large six-cup muffin tins.

In a medium bowl or large measuring cup, whisk together the egg whites, sour cream, passion fruit purée, and vanilla until smooth.

In the bowl of a stand mixer fitted with the paddle attachment, combine the flour, sugar, baking powder, and salt. Start the mixer on low speed and add the butter, one piece at a time, until the mixture resembles coarse sand.

With the mixer still on low, slowly pour in about half of the wet ingredients, then increase the speed to medium and beat until incorporated, about 30 seconds. Return to low speed and add the remaining wet ingredients, mixing until just combined. Scrape down the sides of the bowl, add the poppy seeds, and give the batter a few final stirs with a spatula to ensure everything is well mixed.

Divide the batter evenly among the muffin cups, filling each about ½ inch [12 mm] below the top. Gently tap the muffin tin on the counter to release any air bubbles.

Bake for 22 to 27 minutes, rotating the pans halfway through. The muffins are done when a toothpick inserted in the center comes out with only a few moist crumbs, or when the tops spring back lightly to the touch.

For Preparing the Icing

While the muffins are baking, whisk together the confectioners' sugar, 2 tablespoons of passion fruit purée, melted butter, and vanilla. Adjust the consistency by adding more purée, 1 tablespoon at a time, until you achieve a smooth, pourable glaze.

Once the muffins are done, transfer the tins to a wire rack and let the muffins cool for 5 minutes. Pour half of the icing over the tops of the muffins while they're still warm, allowing it to seep into each muffin. Carefully remove the muffins from the tins, transfer them to a wire rack set over parchment paper, and pour the remaining icing on top. Sprinkle with a few more poppy seeds for an extra touch.

These muffins are best enjoyed the same day they're made, but they can be stored in an airtight container at room temperature for up to 2 days.

Variations:

Lemon Poppyseed
Replace the passion fruit purée with ½ cup [119 g] of whole milk and ¼ cup [59 g] of fresh lemon juice. Add 1 tablespoon of lemon zest to the batter, and swap the passion fruit purée in the icing with lemon juice.

Orange Cranberry
Replace the passion fruit purée with ½ cup [119 g] of whole milk and ¼ cup [59 g] of orange juice. Add 1 tablespoon of orange zest along with the sugar, and fold in 2 oz [57 g] of chopped fresh or thawed cranberries for a festive twist.

Meyer Lemon & White Chocolate Scones

Ingredients

For the Scones:

- Granulated sugar: 1/3 cup [65 g], plus more for sprinkling
- Meyer lemon zest: 2 tablespoons
- All-purpose flour: 2 1/4 cups [320 g], plus more for dusting
- Baking powder: 1 tablespoon
- Salt: 1/2 teaspoon
- Crème fraîche (or sour cream): 1/2 cup [119 g]
- Fresh Meyer lemon juice: 1/4 cup [59 g]
- Egg: 1 large, plus 1 large egg yolk
- Natural vanilla extract: 1 teaspoon
- Unsalted butter: 12 tablespoons [1 1/2 sticks or 169 g], cut into 12 pieces and placed in the freezer for 10 minutes
- White chocolate: 2 oz [55 g], chopped into small pieces
- Heavy cream: for brushing

For the Lemon Glaze:

- Confectioners' sugar: 1 1/2 cups [179 g]
- Fresh Meyer lemon juice: 2 to 4 tablespoons [30 to 59 g]
- Unsalted butter: 1 tablespoon, melted

Makes 8 Scones

Directions

For the Scones

1. Position a rack in the middle of the oven and preheat it to 400°F [200°C]. Stack two baking sheets and line the top one with parchment paper. This double layering helps keep the bottoms of the scones from browning too quickly, ensuring even baking.
2. In a large bowl, combine the sugar and Meyer lemon zest. Use your fingers to rub the zest into the sugar until the mixture is fragrant and the zest releases its oils. This step really brings out the lemon flavor, giving the scones a wonderful aroma.
3. Add the flour, baking powder, and salt to the bowl, whisking to combine. In a separate medium bowl, whisk together the crème fraîche, lemon juice, egg, egg yolk, and vanilla extract until smooth.
4. Take the chilled butter pieces from the freezer and add them to the dry ingredients. Use a pastry cutter or your fingers to cut the butter into the flour mixture until it resembles coarse crumbs with pea-sized bits of butter scattered throughout. Gently fold in the wet ingredients with a spatula until just combined, being careful not to overmix. Finally, fold in the chopped white chocolate.
5. Transfer the dough to a lightly floured surface and gently knead it four to six times until it just comes together. Pat the dough into a 12-inch [30.5 cm] square. Fold it in thirds, like a letter, and then in thirds again to form a smaller square. Place this dough square on a floured plate or sheet pan and chill in the freezer for 10 minutes.
6. After chilling, return the dough to the floured surface, roll it out into a 12-inch [30.5 cm] square again, and fold it in thirds once more. Roll it out into a rectangle measuring about 12 by 4 inches [30.5 by 10 cm]. Using a sharp knife, cut the dough into four equal rectangles, and then cut each rectangle diagonally into two triangles, yielding eight scones.
7. Place the scones on the prepared baking sheet, brush the tops with a little heavy cream, and sprinkle with granulated sugar. Bake for 18 to 25 minutes, rotating halfway through, until the tops and bottoms are golden brown. Transfer the baking sheet to a wire rack and let the scones cool for about 5 minutes.

For the Lemon Glaze

While the scones are cooling, prepare the glaze. In a medium bowl, whisk together the confectioners' sugar, 2 tablespoons of Meyer lemon juice, and melted butter until smooth. If you prefer a thinner consistency, add more lemon juice, one tablespoon at a time.

Once the scones are cool, drizzle or brush the glaze generously over the tops, letting it set before serving. The glaze adds a delightful tangy sweetness that perfectly complements the richness of the scones.

Make It Early

If you'd like to prepare these scones ahead of time, cut the unbaked scones into triangles and place them on a sheet pan. Freeze until solid, then transfer to a freezer-safe bag. They'll keep in the freezer for up to 2 weeks. When ready to bake, simply add a few extra minutes to the baking time.

Sweet Blueberry Morning Buns

Makes 12 buns

Ingredients

For the Blueberry Jam:
- Blueberries (fresh or frozen): 1 1/2 cups (211 g)
- Granulated sugar: 1/4 cup (49 g)
- Salt: a pinch
- Natural vanilla extract: 1 teaspoon
- Fresh lemon juice: 1 teaspoon (optional)

For the Buns:
- All-purpose flour: for dusting
- Fluffy Sweet Dough: 1 recipe (chapter 1), chilled
- Unsalted butter: 2 tablespoons, melted, plus more for greasing the pan
- Cozy Crumble Topping: 1/2 recipe (chapter 5)

For the Icing:
- Cream cheese: 2 oz (57 g), at room temperature
- Fresh lemon juice or water: 2-4 tablespoons (30-59 g)
- Unsalted butter: 1 tablespoon, melted
- Natural vanilla extract: 1/2 teaspoon
- Salt: a pinch
- Confectioners' sugar: 1 1/2 cups (179 g)

Directions

For the Blueberry Jam
In a medium saucepan over medium heat, simmer the blueberries, granulated sugar, and salt for about 20-30 minutes, stirring frequently, until the blueberries have broken down and the jam has thickened. You'll know it's done when the jam clings to a wooden spoon. Remove from heat, stir in the vanilla, and let it cool to room temperature. Taste the jam, and if it needs a little brightness, add the lemon juice a bit at a time.

For Prepare the Buns
Line a baking sheet with parchment paper. Flour a work surface and knead the chilled Sweet Dough 10-12 times. Shape it into a ball, lightly dust the top with flour, cover with a kitchen towel, and let it come to room temperature. Grease a 9x13-inch (23x33 cm) pan. Roll out the dough into a 16x12-inch (40.5x30.5 cm) rectangle. Brush with melted butter and spread ¾ cup (225 g) of the blueberry jam evenly over the top. Starting from a long edge, roll the dough tightly into a log, pinching the seam to seal.
Place the log seam-side down on the prepared baking sheet and refrigerate for 15 minutes. Remove from the fridge, then use scissors or a sharp knife to cut the log into 12 equal pieces. Arrange the pieces in the prepared pan with the cut sides facing up. Cover loosely with plastic wrap and let rise at room temperature until doubled in size, 1-1 ½ hours.

Bake
Adjust an oven rack to the middle position and preheat the oven to 350°F (180°C). Remove the plastic wrap, generously sprinkle the tops of the buns with streusel, pressing it gently to adhere. Bake the buns for 27-32 minutes, rotating the pan halfway through, until they're golden brown.

Make the Icing
While the buns are baking, whisk the cream cheese, 2 tablespoons lemon juice, melted butter, vanilla, and salt in a medium bowl until smooth. Add the confectioners' sugar and mix until fully incorporated. For a thinner icing, add more lemon juice, one tablespoon at a time, until you reach your desired consistency.

Assemble
When the buns are done baking, transfer them to a wire rack and let cool for 10-15 minutes. Drizzle the icing over the warm buns. These buns are best enjoyed on the same day but can be stored in an airtight container at room temperature.

Note:
For a burst of blueberry flavor, pulse ¼ cup (8 g) of freeze-dried blueberries in a food processor until powdered, and add them to the saucepan along with the fresh or frozen berries when making the jam.

Dreamy Coconut Cardamom Cupcakes

Ingredients

For the Coconut Cupcakes:

- Large egg whites: 1 scant cup [211 g], from 6 or 7 eggs, at room temperature
- Coconut milk: 1 cup [240 g], at room temperature
- Homemade French Crème Fraîche (chapter 5) or sour cream: 1/2 cup [119 g], at room temperature
- Natural vanilla extract: 1 tablespoon
- Coconut extract: 1 teaspoon
- All-purpose flour: 2 3/4 cups [391 g]

For the Cardamom Buttercream:

- Unsalted butter: 1 cup [2 sticks or 227 g], at room temperature
- Cream cheese: 8 oz [226 g], at room temperature
- Light corn syrup: 2 tablespoons
- Ground cardamom: 1 teaspoon
- Salt: a pinch
- Confectioners' sugar: 4 1/2 cups [540 g]
- Natural vanilla extract: 2 teaspoons

For Assembly:

- Unsweetened coconut flakes: for sprinkling

Makes 12 Large or 24 Small Cupcakes

Directions

For Make the Cupcakes

1. Preheat the oven: Set an oven rack in the middle and preheat to 350°F [180°C]. Grease two six-cup popover pans or line two standard 12-cup muffin tins with paper liners.
2. Mix the wet ingredients: In a medium bowl or liquid measuring cup, whisk together the egg whites, coconut milk, crème fraîche, vanilla, and coconut extract.
3. Combine the dry ingredients: In the bowl of a stand mixer fitted with a paddle attachment, combine the flour, granulated sugar, baking powder, and salt. With the mixer running on low speed, add the butter one piece at a time, mixing until the texture resembles coarse sand.
4. Add the wet ingredients: Slowly add a little more than half of the wet ingredients to the mixer on low speed. Increase to medium speed, mixing until combined. Add the remaining wet ingredients, mixing until just combined. Increase the speed to medium again and beat for 20 seconds to smooth the batter.
5. Fill the pans: Divide the batter among the cupcake cups, filling each about three-quarters full. Gently tap the pans to release air bubbles. Bake for 16-22 minutes, until golden brown and a toothpick inserted in the center comes out clean. Transfer to a wire rack to cool for 15 minutes, then remove cupcakes from the pans and let them cool completely.

For Make the Cardamom Buttercream

1. Cream the butter: In a stand mixer fitted with a paddle attachment, beat the butter on medium speed until creamy, about 2-3 minutes. Add the cream cheese, corn syrup, cardamom, and salt, and mix until smooth.
2. Add the confectioners' sugar: Reduce the mixer speed to low and gradually add the confectioners' sugar. Once incorporated, add the vanilla, mixing until smooth and creamy.

For Assemble

Generously frost each cupcake with the cardamom buttercream and sprinkle with coconut flakes for a delicate, snowy finish. Cupcakes can be covered and stored in the refrigerator for up to 24 hours. Bring to room temperature before serving.

Flaky Croissant Muffins

Ingredients

For the Muffins:

- All-purpose flour: for dusting
- Easy croissant dough: 1 recipe (chapter 1)
- Unsalted butter: 3 tablespoons, melted, plus more for greasing the pans
- Granulated sugar: 3/4 cup [149 g], plus more for sprinkling in the pan and rolling

Optional:

- Heavenly Pastry Cream (chapter 5)

Makes 12 Muffins

Directions

1. **Prepare the Muffin Pans:** Butter the wells of two large six-cup popover pans and generously dust each with sugar. Line a sheet pan with parchment paper.
2. **Shape the Dough:** Place the Cheater's Croissant Dough on a lightly floured work surface and cut it into six equal pieces. Put the dough on the prepared sheet pan, cover loosely with plastic wrap, and refrigerate.
3. **Roll and Fill:** Take one piece of dough at a time, rolling it out as long, wide, and thin as you can—about 8 by 18 inches. Brush the piece with melted butter and sprinkle with a generous tablespoon of sugar. Then, starting from a short edge, roll up the dough into a log and cut it in half lengthwise to reveal the beautiful layers.
4. **Create the Croissants:** Fold the dough into a horseshoe shape and twist one side of the dough over the other, making a lovely loop. Place the ends of the dough into one well of the prepared popover pan, ensuring the ends are resting on the bottom while the top loop sticks out slightly. Repeat with the remaining dough.
5. **Let Them Rise:** Cover the pans loosely with plastic wrap and let the dough rise at room temperature until doubled in size, about 2 to 3 hours. For the best flavor, you can also let them rise overnight in the refrigerator.

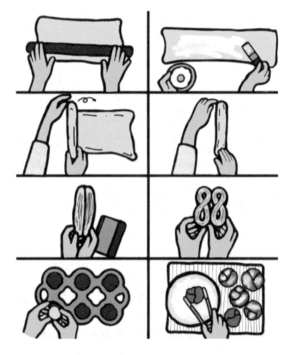

6. **Bake:**

    Preheat your oven to 400°F (200°C). Remove the plastic wrap from the pans and bake the croissants for 25 to 35 minutes, until they are golden brown. Let them sit in the pans for 1 to 2 minutes before flipping them onto the prepared sheet pan.

7. **Finish Up:**

    Roll each croissant in granulated sugar, if desired, and place them on a wire rack to cool. For an extra touch of sweetness, fill each croissant with pastry cream, if desired. Use a piping bag to gently fill the top of each croissant. Enjoy these delightful treats the same day they are made!

This recipe offers a warm, inviting experience perfect for sharing with friends and family on a cozy morning. If you need any more adjustments or additional recipes, just let me know!

Decadent Hot Chocolate Cake

Ingredients

- Sour cream: 1/2 cup [119 g], at room temperature
- Whole milk: 1/2 cup [119 g], at room temperature
- Canola oil: 1/2 cup [112 g]
- Eggs: 3 large, at room temperature
- Natural vanilla extract: 1 teaspoon
- All-purpose flour: 2 cups [284 g]
- Granulated sugar: 1 cup [199 g]
- Light brown sugar: 1 cup [199 g]
- Dutch-process cocoa powder: 3/4 cup [75 g]
- Baking soda: 2 teaspoons
- Baking powder: 1 teaspoon
- Salt: 1 teaspoon
- Strong, freshly brewed coffee: 1 cup [240 g], hot

For the Marshmallow Fluff Filling:
- Unsalted butter: 8 tablespoons [1 stick or 114 g], at room temperature
- Salt: a pinch
- Confectioners' sugar: 1 cup [119 g]
- Fluffy Homemade Marshmallow Cream (chapter 5): 2 cups [279 g] Heavy cream: 2 tablespoons

For the Ganache:
- Semisweet or bittersweet chocolate: 8 oz [226 g]
- Heavy cream: 1/2 cup [119 g]
- Fluffy Homemade Marshmallow (chapter 5): cut into cubes and toasted

Makes 8 to 12 servings

Directions

To Prepare the Cake

1. Preheat your oven to 350°F (180°C) and adjust an oven rack to the middle position. Grease a tube pan (without a removable bottom) and line the bottom with parchment paper, using a hole cut in the middle for the tube.
2. In a medium bowl or liquid measuring cup, whisk together the sour cream, milk, oil, eggs, and vanilla.
3. In the bowl of a stand mixer fitted with a paddle, whisk together the flour, granulated and brown sugars, cocoa powder, baking soda, baking powder, and salt by hand.
4. With the mixer running on low speed, slowly add the milk mixture. Increase the speed to medium and beat until combined, about 20 to 30 seconds.
5. Slowly pour the hot coffee into the batter and mix on low speed until just combined. Use a spatula to ensure everything is well mixed.
6. Pour the batter evenly into the prepared pan and bake for 25 to 35 minutes, until a wooden skewer or toothpick comes out with just a few crumbs.
7. Transfer the cake to a wire rack and let it cool in the pan for 1 hour. Turn the cake out onto the rack, remove the parchment paper, and let cool completely. Wrap the cake in plastic wrap and chill for at least 2 hours and up to overnight.

To Prepare the Filling

1. In the bowl of a stand mixer fitted with a paddle, beat the butter and salt on medium speed until creamy, about 1 minute. Add the confectioners' sugar and beat again until smooth and creamy, 3 to 4 minutes.
2. Scrape down the sides and add the marshmallow fluff, beating on low speed until well blended. Transfer the filling to a bowl and cover. Chill in the refrigerator for at least 2 hours and up to overnight.

To Fill the Cake

1. Set the cake rounded-side up on a sheet pan. Using a small paring knife, make a tunnel in the cake by cutting out small curved rectangles (about 2 in long by 1 in wide [5 by 2.5 cm]) into the top of the cake following the curve of the entire cake, directly in the center. Save the pieces of cut-out cake. The tunnel should go down a little more than half the depth of the cake.
2. Once you go around the entire cake, spoon the chilled marshmallow filling into the tunnel, filling it halfway (you may have some leftover fluff). Cut off half of the inside of each piece of cut-out rectangle. Replace the cake pieces in the tunnel over the fluff, covering all of it.
3. Turn the cake over onto a serving plate so the cut-out side is on the bottom. Cover the cake loosely with plastic wrap and chill for 1 hour.

To Assemble

1. Remove the cake from the fridge and pour the ganache over the top, letting it drip down the sides. Let the ganache set until just tacky, then add the toasted marshmallows to the top.

Sprinkle Celebration Cake

Ingredients

- Large egg whites: 1 scant cup (211 g), from 6 or 7 eggs, at room temperature
- Whole milk: 1 cup (240 g), at room temperature
- Crème fraîche or sour cream: 1/2 cup (119 g), at room temperature
- Natural vanilla extract: 1 tablespoon
- All-purpose flour: 2 3/4 cups (391 g), plus more for coating the pans
- Granulated sugar: 2 cups (399 g)
- Baking powder: 4 teaspoons
- Salt: 1 teaspoon
- Unsalted butter: 1 cup (2 sticks or 227 g), at room temperature, cut into 1-inch (2.5 cm) pieces
- Sprinkles: 3/4 cup (114 g)

Cream Cheese Icing Ingredients:

- Unsalted butter: 1 cup (2 sticks or 227 g), at room temperature
- Cream cheese: 8 oz (226 g), at room temperature
- Light corn syrup: 2 tablespoons
- Salt: a pinch
- Confectioners' sugar: 4 1/2 cups (540 g)
- Natural vanilla extract: 1 tablespoon

Makes 8 to 12 servings

Directions

For the Cake:

1. Preheat your oven to 350°F (180°C) and prepare two 8 by 2 in (20 by 5 cm) round cake pans by buttering and flouring them generously. You can also line the bottoms with parchment paper for easy removal later.
2. In a medium bowl or liquid measuring cup, whisk together the egg whites, milk, crème fraîche, and vanilla. In a stand mixer fitted with a paddle attachment, mix the flour, granulated sugar, baking powder, and salt by hand.
3. With the mixer running on low speed, add the butter one piece at a time, mixing until the mixture resembles coarse sand. Then, slowly add a little more than half of the wet ingredients, increasing the speed to medium and mixing until fully incorporated, about 30 seconds.
4. With the mixer still on low speed, add the rest of the wet ingredients, mixing until just combined. Scrape down the sides and bottom of the bowl, and add the sprinkles, gently folding them in.
5. Divide the batter between the prepared pans and smooth the tops. Gently tap the pans on the counter to help release any air bubbles. Bake for 30 to 38 minutes, rotating the pans halfway through until the cakes are golden brown. A wooden skewer or toothpick inserted into the center should come out with just a few crumbs.
6. Transfer the cakes to a wire rack and let cool in the pans for 30 minutes. Turn the cakes out onto the rack, remove the parchment paper, and let them cool completely. Once cooled, the cakes can be wrapped in plastic and refrigerated overnight. Unfrosted cakes can also be frozen for up to one week.

For the Icing:

1. In a stand mixer fitted with a paddle, beat the butter and cream cheese on medium speed until light yellow and creamy, about 3 minutes. Add the corn syrup and salt, mixing until well combined.
2. Lower the speed to low and gradually add the confectioners' sugar. Increase the speed to medium and mix until smooth and creamy, stopping to scrape down the sides of the bowl as necessary, 2 to 3 minutes. Add the vanilla and mix again on low speed until combined.

To Assemble:

1. Place one cake layer on a turntable or serving plate. With an offset spatula, spread the top with 1 cup (320 g) of icing. Place the second layer on top and frost with the remaining icing. The cake can be covered and stored in the refrigerator for up to 24 hours. Remember to bring the cake to room temperature before serving.

Notes:

- Large sprinkles work best in the batter as smaller ones tend to melt and bleed too much.
- This cake can also be made in a 9 by 13 in (23 by 33 cm) pan, and you can omit the sprinkles for a beautiful white cake.

Quick and Easy Puff Pastry

Ingredients

- Unsalted butter: 1 1/2 cups [3 sticks or 339 g], cut into 20 pieces
- Ice water: 1 cup [240 g]
- Fresh lemon juice: 1/2 teaspoon
- All-purpose flour: 2 cups [284 g], plus more for dusting
- Granulated sugar: 1 tablespoon
- Salt: 1/2 teaspoon

Makes 8 to 12 servings

Directions

1. Prepare the Butter: Start by placing the butter pieces in a small bowl and transferring it to the freezer for about 5 to 10 minutes. This step ensures that your butter stays cold and will create those lovely layers we all adore.
2. Mix the Wet Ingredients: In a liquid measuring cup, combine ¼ cup [59 g] of the ice water with the fresh lemon juice. This will add a little brightness to your pastry.
3. Combine Dry Ingredients: In the bowl of a stand mixer fitted with a paddle attachment, mix together the flour, sugar, and salt on low speed. This step is crucial as it helps to evenly distribute the dry ingredients.
4. Incorporate the Butter: Add the chilled butter to the dry mixture and mix on low speed until the butter is slightly incorporated. You want the butter to be smashed and in varying sizes, with about half of it remaining intact. This variation will help create those delightful layers in your pastry.
5. Add Wet Ingredients: Next, take that lemony ice water mixture you prepared earlier and mix it in on low speed until the dough starts to hold together and looks a bit shaggy. If the dough is still quite dry, don't fret! Just add more ice water, one tablespoon at a time, until it begins to form.
6. Shape the Dough: Transfer the dough to a lightly floured work surface and gently flatten it into a square. Gather any loose or dry pieces that may have fallen off and place them on top of the square. Gently fold the dough over itself and then flatten it again into a square. This gentle folding process is essential as it starts to build the layers.
7. Repeat the Turns: Repeat this folding process four to six times until all the loose pieces are worked into the dough, being careful not to overwork it. After the final fold, flatten the dough into a 6-inch [15 cm] square. Transfer it to a floured sheet pan or plate and sprinkle a little flour on top. Cover the dough with plastic wrap and chill it in the refrigerator for 20 minutes.
8. Rolling Out: Once chilled, return the dough to the lightly floured work surface. Roll it out into an 8 by 16-inch [20 by 40.5 cm] rectangle. If the dough sticks, sprinkle more flour underneath. Once rolled out, brush any excess flour off and, using a bench scraper, fold the short ends of the dough over the middle, creating three layers, much like a business letter. This is your first turn!
9. Flipping and Folding: If your dough looks a bit shaggy, don't worry; it will smooth out as you continue rolling. Flip the dough over (seam-side down), give it a quarter turn, and roll away from you to create a 6 by 16-inch [15 by 40.5 cm] rectangle. Again, fold the short ends over the middle for your second turn. Sprinkle flour on top before returning it to the sheet pan for another chill in the fridge for 20 minutes.
10. Final Touches: Repeat the folding and rolling process, creating your third and fourth turns, gently compressing the layers together with a rolling pin. Wrap the dough tightly in plastic wrap and chill for at least 1 hour before using, or keep refrigerated for up to 2 days.

This Quick and Easy Puff Pastry will open up a world of culinary possibilities for you, from sweet treats to savory delights. With each flaky layer, you'll taste the love and care that went into making it. Enjoy your baking adventure!

5
Extra Delights

Golden Caramel Shards: a Sweet, Crunchy Surprise

Ingredients

- Granulated sugar: 1/2 cup [100 g]
- Light corn syrup: 1/4 cup [79 g]
- Water: 2 tablespoons
- Salt: 1/4 teaspoon
- Natural vanilla extract: 2 teaspoons

Makes 2 cups (221 g)

Picture this: the satisfying crunch of golden caramel shards gracefully melting into your desserts, infusing each bite with a touch of sweetness and magic.

These caramel shards are the ultimate way to introduce an unforgettable texture contrast to your treats. Whether you're decorating a cake, topping off ice cream, or adding flair to pastries, these delightful shards bring an irresistible crunch that elevates your desserts to a whole new level. Trust me, once you try them, you'll find countless ways to incorporate these golden wonders into your baking repertoire!

Directions

1. Prepare your base: Start by placing a sheet of parchment paper on a baking sheet. This will be where your caramel transforms into a fragile golden sheet, ready to be broken into delicious pieces.
2. Gently combine the ingredients: In a heavy-bottomed saucepan, gently stir together the sugar, corn syrup, water, and a pinch of salt. Stir slowly, trying to avoid any sugar crystals forming along the sides of the pan. This little trick will help your caramel stay smooth and silky.
3. Bring to a boil and watch the magic happen: Cover the pan and let the mixture begin to boil over medium-high heat. After about 3-5 minutes, remove the lid and watch as the mixture turns into a clear golden liquid. It's a moment of pure alchemy!
4. Achieve the golden hue: With the lid off, continue cooking until the caramel reaches a light golden shade, similar to honey, which should take about 4-5 minutes. At this point, the temperature should be around 300°F (150°C). Lower the heat slightly and cook a bit longer, until it reaches 350°F (180°C) on your thermometer and takes on a deeper golden color. Patience is the secret to perfect caramel!
5. Add a touch of vanilla: Remove the pan from the heat and stir in the vanilla extract carefully. This little detail adds a warm, fragrant note that will make your caramel even more inviting.
6. Pour and cool: Carefully pour the hot caramel onto the prepared baking sheet, tilting it gently to spread the caramel into a thin, even layer about ¼ inch (6 mm) thick. Allow the caramel to cool completely, hardening into a beautiful golden sheet.
7. Break into pieces and store: Once the caramel is fully set, use a knife to cut it into larger shards or break it into smaller pieces using a food processor. Store these golden shards in an airtight container at room temperature, where they'll stay crisp for up to 2 weeks, ready to add a magical crunch to your desserts!

Fluffy Homemade Marshmallows

Ingredients

- Confectioners' sugar: 3/4 cup (90 g)
- Cornstarch: 1/4 cup (28 g)
- Gelatin: 5 teaspoons
- Cold water: 1/2 cup (119 g)
- Room-temperature water: 1/2 cup (119 g)
- Granulated sugar: 2 cups (399 g)
- Light corn syrup: 1/4 cup (79 g)
- Salt: 1/4 teaspoon
- Egg whites: 2 large, at room temperature
- Cream of tartar: 1/4 teaspoon
- Natural vanilla extract: 1 tablespoon

Make 24 Large or 48 Small Marshmallows

Making marshmallows at home is truly a revelation—they're far better than anything you'll find on a store shelf. These homemade marshmallows are soft, airy, and toast to perfection, forming a sweet, amber crust that's simply magical. Once you've tried them, you'll never look back!

Directions

1. Lightly grease a 9 x 13 inch (23 x 33 cm) baking pan. In a small bowl, whisk together the confectioners' sugar and cornstarch; set aside.
2. In another small bowl, bloom the gelatin by sprinkling it over the cold water. In a medium, heavy-bottomed saucepan, combine the granulated sugar, room-temperature water, corn syrup, and salt. Heat over medium-high until it reaches 240°F (115°C), about 4-5 minutes. Remove from heat, then whisk in the bloomed gelatin until fully dissolved.
3. In the bowl of a stand mixer fitted with the whisk attachment, beat the egg whites and cream of tartar on medium-high until soft peaks form, about 2-3 minutes. With the mixer on low speed, carefully pour the hot sugar syrup down the side of the bowl (avoiding the whisk). Increase the speed to medium-high and whip until the mixture is thick, glossy, and cool to the touch, about 8-10 minutes. Add the vanilla and beat just until combined.
4. Pour the marshmallow mixture into the prepared pan, using an offset spatula to smooth the top. Sift 2-3 tablespoons of the confectioners' sugar mixture over the surface. Let sit, uncovered, at room temperature overnight until firm.
5. The next day, remove the marshmallow slab from the pan and cut it into squares with a lightly oiled knife or scissors. Dust the marshmallows with more of the confectioners' sugar mixture, tossing a few at a time to prevent sticking. Store the marshmallows in an airtight container at room temperature for up to one week.

Variation:

Minty Twist: Peppermint Marshmallows: For a refreshing twist, add 2 teaspoons of pure peppermint extract (or more to taste) along with the vanilla. A few drops of pink or green food coloring make these marshmallows extra fun for the holidays!

Homemade Caramel Sauce

Ingredients

- Granulated sugar: 1 1/4 cups (249 g)
- Water: 1/3 cup (79 g)
- Light corn syrup: 2 tablespoons
- Salt: 1/2 teaspoon
- Heavy cream: 1/2 cup (119 g)
- Unsalted butter: 5 tablespoons (70 g), cut into 5 pieces
- Natural vanilla extract: 1 tablespoon

Make 1½ Cups (511 g)

There's something truly magical about making caramel from scratch. While store-bought caramel can do in a pinch, a homemade version brings a depth of flavor and richness that simply can't be matched. This caramel is silky, deeply golden, and has just the right balance of sweet and buttery goodness. Drizzle it over ice cream, use it as a dip for apples, or simply enjoy a spoonful on its own—no judgment here!

Directions

1. In a large, heavy-bottom saucepan (choose a deep one, as the caramel will bubble up as it cooks), combine the sugar, water, corn syrup, and salt. Stir very gently to ensure everything is mixed, being careful to avoid getting any sugar crystals on the sides of the pan.
2. Cover the pan and heat over medium-high until the sugar has melted and the mixture is clear, about 3-5 minutes. Once the sugar is dissolved, uncover the pan and let the mixture cook until it reaches a light golden color, which should take about 4-5 more minutes.
3. Turn down the heat to medium and continue cooking until the caramel turns a rich, deep amber color. Use an instant-read thermometer if you have one—the caramel should reach 340°F (170°C).
4. Carefully remove the pan from the heat and slowly add the heavy cream. Be cautious, as the cream will cause the caramel to bubble vigorously. Once the bubbling settles, add in the butter pieces one at a time, stirring until each piece melts fully into the caramel.
5. Finally, add the vanilla and stir gently to combine everything into a smooth, luscious sauce. Let the caramel cool, then transfer it to an airtight container. Store it in the refrigerator for up to 2 weeks, ready for whenever a touch of sweetness is needed.

Variation:

Salted Caramel: For a salted caramel twist, add ½ teaspoon of fleur de sel just after removing the pan from the heat. Stir until the salt dissolves, giving the caramel a subtle, irresistible hint of saltiness that complements its sweetness perfectly.

Ice Cream
Without the Churn

Ingredients

- Sweetened condensed milk: one 14 oz (397 g) can
- Natural vanilla extract: 1 tablespoon
- Vanilla bean seeds: from 1 vanilla bean (optional)
- Salt: 1/4 teaspoon
- Cream cheese: 2 oz (57 g), at room temperature
- Heavy cream: 2 cups (240 g)

Makes about 4
cups (959 g)

There's something so wonderful about no-churn ice cream recipes; they're a lovely alternative to traditional homemade ice cream, taking less time and requiring no special equipment. Here's my basic recipe—a simple, delightful treat—along with a few fun variations that pair beautifully with other creations in this book.

Directions

1. In a large bowl, whisk together the sweetened condensed milk, vanilla, vanilla bean seeds (if using), and salt until smooth and fragrant. In the bowl of a stand mixer fitted with the whisk attachment, beat the cream cheese on medium speed until creamy and smooth. Lower the speed and slowly add the heavy cream, mixing until fully combined. Increase the speed to medium-high and whip until stiff peaks form, about 3 to 4 minutes.
2. Gently fold half of the whipped cream mixture into the sweetened condensed milk mixture until completely combined. With a rubber spatula, carefully fold in the remaining whipped cream mixture, ensuring the texture stays light and airy. Pour the mixture into a 9 x 4 in (23 x 10 cm) Pullman loaf pan with a lid and freeze until firm, about 6 hours, or store in the freezer for up to 1 week.
3. Note: If you don't have a Pullman pan with a lid, a standard 9 in (23 cm) loaf pan covered with plastic wrap will work just as well.

Variations:

- **Chocolate No-Churn Ice Cream:** Melt 8 oz (226 g) of bittersweet or semisweet chocolate. Pour 5 oz (142 g) onto a parchment-lined sheet pan and freeze until solid, about 10 to 15 minutes. Stir the remaining 3 oz (85 g) of melted chocolate into the sweetened condensed milk mixture. Chop the frozen chocolate into small pieces and fold them into the ice cream mixture before transferring it to the loaf pan.

- **Coffee No-Churn Ice Cream:** Add 1/2 cup (119 g) of room-temperature brewed espresso or strong coffee and 1/2 teaspoon ground espresso to the sweetened condensed milk mixture.

- **Pumpkin Spice No-Churn Ice Cream:** Add 3/4 cup (168 g) unsweetened pumpkin purée, 1/2 teaspoon ground cinnamon, 1/4 teaspoon ground ginger, 1/4 teaspoon freshly grated nutmeg, and a pinch of ground cloves to the sweetened condensed milk mixture.

- **Salted Caramel No-Churn Ice Cream:** Prepare the base ice cream as directed, then pour half of the mixture into the pan and swirl in 1/2 cup (179 g) Homemade Caramel Sauce (chapter 5 - The variation Salted Caramel). Use a knife to gently swirl the caramel through the ice cream. Pour in the remaining ice cream mixture, add another 1/2 cup of caramel on top, and swirl again. Freeze as directed.

- **Blood Orange No-Churn Ice Cream:** Add 1/2 cup (119 g) blood orange juice, 1 tablespoon triple sec, and 2 teaspoons grated blood orange zest to the sweetened condensed milk mixture.

- **Candy Cane No-Churn Ice Cream:** Stir in 1/2 cup (100 g) crushed candy canes and 1 teaspoon peppermint extract (adjust to taste) into the sweetened condensed milk mixture.

Heavenly Pastry Cream

Ingredients

- Egg yolks: 5 large, at room temperature
- Granulated sugar: 1 1/4 cups [249 g]
- Salt: 1/4 teaspoon
- Vanilla bean seeds: from 1 vanilla bean (reserve the pod)
- Cornstarch: 1/4 cup [28 g]
- Whole milk: 1 cup [240 g]
- Heavy cream: 1 cup [240 g]
- Unsalted butter: 1 tablespoon
- Natural vanilla extract: 2 teaspoons

Make about 2 cups (449 g)

This pastry cream is one of those versatile delights that can turn any dessert into something extraordinary. With its smooth, delicate flavor, it's perfect for filling cakes, tarts, or even small homemade treats. For an extra special touch, try whipping it with a bit of room-temperature butter to create a light, fluffy mousse—ideal for decorating or filling. This recipe yields a generous amount of sweet indulgence, ready to enhance your favorite desserts!

Directions

1. Prepare the Cream Base: In the bowl of a stand mixer fitted with a paddle, beat the egg yolks on low speed. With the mixer running, slowly add the sugar, followed by the salt and vanilla bean seeds. Increase the speed to medium-high and beat until the mixture is thick, pale, and creamy, about 5 minutes. Scrape down the sides of the bowl, add the cornstarch, and mix on low speed until combined.
2. Warm the Liquids: In a heavy-bottomed saucepan over medium-low heat, warm the milk, heavy cream, and reserved vanilla bean pod, stirring gently until the mixture is just about to simmer. Remove the vanilla bean pod, and slowly pour the warm liquid into the egg mixture while mixing on low speed.
3. Cook the Pastry Cream: Pour the egg mixture back into the saucepan and cook over medium-low heat, stirring constantly with a wooden spoon. The cream will start to thicken, transforming into a smooth and glossy texture, about 5–7 minutes. Once the cream has thickened beautifully, remove it from the heat and strain it through a fine-mesh sieve into a medium bowl to ensure perfect smoothness.
4. Add the Final Flavors: While the cream is still warm, stir in the butter and vanilla extract until fully melted and incorporated. Transfer the pastry cream to a bowl and cover it with plastic wrap, ensuring the wrap is in direct contact with the surface to prevent a skin from forming.
5. Chill and Store: Let the pastry cream cool in the refrigerator for at least 4 hours or up to 5 days in an airtight container. Use it to fill your favorite desserts, or simply enjoy a spoonful on its own!

Variations:
When adding the sugar to the egg yolks, make sure to mix right away; if left too long, the sugar can create small lumps in the yolks. Stir gently, with care, to achieve a soft and flawless cream.

Sugary Citrus Peel Delights

Ingredients

- Oranges or lemons: 4 large, scrubbed clean
- Granulated sugar: 3 1/2 cups (700 g), plus more for coating
- Water: 3 cups (720 g)
- Light corn syrup: 3 tablespoons

Makes About 3 Cups (449 g)

Making candied citrus peels at home is such a rewarding treat. These little gems add a delightful, sweet crunch to your desserts, drinks, and homemade gifts. Once you learn the trick to removing their bitterness, you'll find yourself making them over and over again.

Directions

1. After scrubbing the citrus well, use a small, sharp knife to cut the peel into large strips. Carefully trim away any excess white pith, then slice the peel into strips about ¼ to ½ inch wide.
2. Bring a large pot of water to a boil over medium-high heat, add the citrus strips, and let them boil for 5 minutes. Drain, refill the pot with fresh water, and repeat this process three times to remove bitterness.
3. In a clean pot, combine the sugar, water, and corn syrup.
4. Bring the mixture to a boil, add the blanched citrus strips, and simmer over medium-low heat until the peels are translucent and the syrup has thickened, about 1½ to 2 hours. Place a wire rack over a parchment-lined baking sheet, and let the candied peels dry at room temperature for 8 hours or overnight.
5. Once dry, toss them in sugar for an extra sparkle and store in an airtight container at room temperature for up to 3 weeks.

Cranberry Sauce with a Holiday Twist

Ingredients

- Granulated sugar: 1/2 cup (100 g)
- Salt: 1/4 teaspoon
- Ground cinnamon: 1/2 teaspoon (optional)
- Water: 1/4 cup (59 g)
- Fresh cranberries: 6 oz (169 g)

Makes About 3 Cups (449 g)

This homemade cranberry jam is a vibrant, sweet-tart addition to your holiday table. It's perfect for Thanksgiving or simply spread on toast for a cozy morning treat.

Directions

In a medium nonreactive saucepan, combine the sugar, salt, cinnamon (if using), and water. Bring the mixture to a boil over medium heat, stirring occasionally until the sugar is dissolved. Add the cranberries and reduce the heat to a simmer. Cook until the cranberries burst and the sauce thickens, about 15-20 minutes. Let it cool to room temperature. Store in an airtight container in the refrigerator for up to 5 days.

Cozy Crumble Topping

Ingredients

- All-purpose flour: 1 1/3 cups (189 g)
- Almond flour: 1 cup (100 g)
- Granulated sugar: 2/3 cup (135 g)
- Light brown sugar: 2/3 cup (135 g)
- Ground cinnamon: 1 tablespoon
- Salt: 1/4 teaspoon

- Unsalted butter: 12 tablespoons (1 1/2 sticks or 169 g), at room temperature, cut into 12 pieces

Makes 4 Cups (499 g)

There's something magical about a warm, crumbly streusel topping. This buttery mix is ideal for sprinkling over muffins, coffee cakes, and more. Keep a batch in your freezer, and you'll always be ready to add a little extra love to your baking.

Directions

- In the bowl of a stand mixer fitted with the paddle attachment, combine the flours, sugars, cinnamon, and salt on low speed.
- Gradually add the butter pieces, mixing until the streusel holds together in large crumbs.
- Store the streusel in an airtight container in the fridge for up to a week, or freeze in a resealable bag for up to a month.

Fluffy Homemade Whipped Cream

Ingredients

- Heavy cream: 1 1/2 cups (359 g)
- Granulated sugar: 2 tablespoons
- Natural vanilla extract: 2 teaspoons
- Salt: a pinch

Makes About 3 Cups (720 g)

There's nothing like fresh whipped cream—it's light, airy, and wonderfully simple to make. Perfect for topping pies, hot cocoa, or just about any dessert.

Directions

1. Ten minutes before whipping, place the mixing bowl and whisk attachment in the freezer to chill.
2. Pour the cream, sugar, vanilla, and salt into the chilled bowl and whisk on low speed for 30 to 45 seconds.
3. Increase to medium speed for another 30 to 45 seconds, then whip on high until soft peaks form, about 30 to 60 seconds.
4. This whipped cream can be made up to 2 hours in advance; store in an airtight container in the fridge until ready to serve.

Homemade French Crème Fraîche

Ingredients

Makes About 4 Cups (959 g)

- Heavy cream: 3 cups (720 g)
- Buttermilk: 3/4 cup (179 g)

Crème fraîche is like sour cream's gentler, silkier cousin. It has a higher fat content and a milder tang, making it perfect for cooking at high temperatures without breaking or curdling. It's also wonderfully versatile—stir it into soups, dollop it on pies, or simply enjoy it with fresh berries.

Directions

- In a large mixing bowl, whisk together the heavy cream and buttermilk until combined. Drape several layers of cheesecloth over the bowl and secure it with a rubber band or string to keep it in place.
- Let the mixture sit at room temperature for 24 hours and up to 3 days until it thickens to a lovely, creamy consistency.
- The time it takes to thicken depends on the temperature in your kitchen; cooler days may require a bit longer, while warmer days may speed things up. Once it reaches the desired thickness, gently stir and transfer it to an airtight container.
- Refrigerate your homemade crème fraîche for up to 1 week.

Note:
Buttermilk contains "good" bacteria that prevent the cream from spoiling while it thickens. It's also acidic enough to deter any unwanted bacteria, keeping your crème fraîche fresh and delicious.

Sugared & Spiced Candied Nuts

Ingredients

- Granulated sugar: 1/2 cup (100 g)
- Water: 2 tablespoons
- Salt: 1/4 teaspoon
- Mixed nuts (walnuts, pecans, almonds, cashews, hazelnuts, or a preferred combination): 2 cups (279 g)

Make about 2 cups (419g)

Directions

1. Begin by lining a baking sheet with parchment paper and setting it aside. In a large skillet over medium heat, combine the sugar, water, and salt. Stir them gently, letting the sugar slowly dissolve into a shimmering, golden syrup.
2. Once the sugar begins to melt, add the nuts, stirring almost constantly. Watch as the nuts start to toast and the sugar begins to caramelize, coating each piece with a beautiful, glossy shine. The smell alone will make your kitchen feel like a warm, inviting haven.
3. When the nuts are fully coated and have a light caramel color, pour them out onto the prepared sheet pan. Spread them out and allow them to cool completely; this gives the caramel a chance to set, creating that irresistible crunch.
4. Once cool, these candied nuts can be enjoyed immediately or chopped up to sprinkle on your favorite desserts. Stored in an airtight container, they'll stay fresh and delicious for up to a week, though they rarely last that long!

Silky Lemon Crud

Ingredients

- Unsalted butter: 8 tablespoons (1 stick or 114 g), at room temperature
- Granulated sugar: 1 1/2 cups (249 g)
- Salt: 1/4 teaspoon
- Egg yolks: 5 large, plus 1 whole egg, at room temperature
- Freshly squeezed lemon juice: 1/3 cup (79 g)

Make about 2 cups (639g)

Directions

- In the bowl of a stand mixer, start by beating the butter on medium speed until it becomes soft and creamy, like the beginning of a perfect frosting. Slowly add the sugar and salt, and beat until well combined and fluffy, about 1-2 minutes.
- Add the egg yolks, one at a time, on low speed, letting each one blend fully into the butter mixture before adding the next. When all the yolks are in, increase the speed to medium, beating until the mixture is smooth and a lovely pale yellow.
- Now, add the whole egg, mixing until it's just combined, followed by the lemon juice. Don't worry if it looks a bit curdled—that's normal at this stage.
- Transfer the mixture to a heavy-bottom saucepan and set it over medium heat. Stir constantly with a spatula, watching as the mixture transforms from liquid to a thick, rich curd, about 10 minutes. You'll know it's ready when it coats the back of a spoon and reaches about 170°F (75°C).
- Strain the curd through a fine-mesh sieve to catch any bits, then transfer it to a bowl. Press plastic wrap directly onto the surface to prevent a skin from forming, and let it cool. Stored in an airtight container in the fridge, this curd will keep for up to five days, ready to add a zesty touch to anything you like.

Variations:

- **Blood Orange Curd:** Swap out the lemon juice with ½ cup (120g) blood orange juice for a sweeter, more aromatic flavor.
- **Passion Fruit Curd:** Replace the lemon juice with ½ cup (120g) passion fruit purée for a tropical twist that brings a sunny, floral note to every spoonful.

Fluffy Homemade Marshmallow Cream

Ingredients

- Egg whites: 4 large
- Cream of tartar: 1/2 teaspoon
- Cold water: 2 tablespoons
- Room temperature water: 1/2 cup (119 g)
- Gelatin: 1 teaspoon
- Corn syrup: 1 cup (320 g)
- Granulated sugar: 1 cup (199 g)
- Salt: 1/4 teaspoon
- Natural vanilla extract: 1 tablespoon

Make about 2 cups (419g)

Directions

1. Whisk egg whites with cream of tartar until soft peaks form.
2. Bloom gelatin in cold water.
3. Heat corn syrup, sugar, water, and salt to 240°F (115°C).
4. Add gelatin to the hot syrup and pour into the egg whites.
5. Whisk until thick and glossy (8-10 minutes), add vanilla, and store in the fridge.

Baking Conversion Chart

Commonly Used Ingredients

- 1 cup flour = 142 g
- 1 cup cocoa powder = 100 g
- 1 cup heavy cream = 240 g
- 1 cup granulated sugar = 200 g
- 1 cup butter (2 sticks) = 227 g
- 1 cup whole milk = 240 g

- 1 cup brown sugar = 200 g
- 1 egg white = 35 g
- 1 cup cream cheese (8 oz) = 226 g
- 1 cup confectioners' sugar = 120 g
- 1 cup sour cream = 240 g

Oven Temperatures

- 300°F = 150°C
- 350°F = 180°C
- 375°F = 190°C
- 400°F = 200°C
- 425°F = 220°C
- 450°F = 230°C

Weights

- 1/2 oz = 14 g
- 3 oz = 85 g
- 8 oz = 226 g
- 1 oz = 28 g
- 3 1/2 oz = 99 g

- 10 oz = 283 g
- 1 1/2 oz = 45 g
- 4 oz = 113 g
- 12 oz = 340 g
- 2 oz = 57 g

- 4 1/2 oz = 128 g
- 16 oz = 455 g
- 2 1/2 oz = 71 g
- 5 oz = 142 g

Conculsion

As I reach the final page of this book, I find myself reflecting on what this season means—the essence of gathering, the joy of sharing, and the simple pleasure of creating something with love. The holidays have a way of bringing us back to what's important, a gentle reminder that amidst life's busyness, it's the moments of connection that stay with us. Whether you're gathering with family, reaching out to friends, or savoring some quiet time by yourself, I hope these recipes bring a sense of comfort and joy to your celebrations.

The world around us can often feel overwhelming, filled with challenges and uncertainties. But the holidays, with their warmth and light, offer us a chance to pause and reset. They remind us that hope can be renewed, that love can be rekindled, and that the smallest acts—like sharing a meal or baking something sweet for someone we care about—can be powerful gestures of kindness. It's in these acts, in these quiet offerings, that we spread peace in our own small ways.

As we close out another year, let's look forward with hearts full of hope. Let us be gentle with ourselves, knowing that each day brings a new chance to learn, to grow, and to love. And let us be kind to one another, reaching out across distances, across differences, to remind each other that we are not alone. In a world that sometimes feels divided, may our kitchens and tables be places of unity, where everyone is welcomed, everyone is valued, and everyone belongs.

This book, I hope, will serve as a companion in those joyful moments—a guide not only to delicious treats but to creating memories filled with love. Let each recipe be a reminder of the good things in life: the laughter shared over a table, the warmth of a kitchen filled with sweet aromas, and the gratitude that fills our hearts when we're together.

So, as you turn this last page, I wish for you a season brimming with peace, laughter, and boundless hope. May the coming year be filled with dreams that inspire you, kindness that lifts you, and love that sustains you. And when you bake these recipes, may you feel the presence of all those who have baked before you, all those who will come after you, and all those who are baking in kitchens around the world, united in the simple joy of sharing something wonderful.

Here's to a New Year filled with peace—for ourselves, for each other, and for the world. May we carry forward the spirit of the season, spreading love and light wherever we go.

Happy holidays to you and yours.

May each day be as sweet as the treats we bake, and may each gathering be filled with love that lingers long after the last crumb has been shared.

Olivia Dowson

Made in the USA
Columbia, SC
18 December 2024

49976214R00050